VIRGIL'S *GEORGICS*

VIRGIL'S *GEORGICS*

Publius Vergilius Maro

A

*Modern English Verse
Translation*

By

SMITH PALMER BOVIE

THE UNIVERSITY OF CHICAGO PRESS

Library of Congress Catalog Number: 56-11264

2-7-57

THE UNIVERSITY OF CHICAGO PRESS, CHICAGO 37
Cambridge University Press, London, N.W. 1, England
The University of Toronto Press, Toronto 5, Canada

© *1956 by The University of Chicago. Published 1956*
Composed and printed by THE UNIVERSITY OF CHICAGO
PRESS, *Chicago, Illinois, U.S.A.*

CONTENTS

INTRODUCTION

I. THE HISTORICAL BACKGROUND

The years during which Virgil was writing the *Georgics* appear, in retrospect, to have been very significant for the future of Rome. By 37 B.C., when Virgil began the composition of this second of his major poetic works, the struggle for power among the various would-be leaders of the Roman world had reached a point of uneasy compromise. The conspirators who had struck down Julius Caesar had been routed and destroyed, and, while minor potential rivals still hovered in the wings, the center of the Roman political stage was occupied by the contrasting figures of Marcus Antonius and Gaius Julius Caesar Octavianus. The Octavian who was destined to triumph over the older man was still, at the moment, more than ready to collaborate with Marc Antony, the veteran of Caesar's campaigns, and to enjoy the prestige of association with the experienced leader staunchly loyal to the memory of Julius Caesar. Fortunately for Octavian, Julius had named him as his heir, thereby establishing a link between the generations, but Antony was still the personification of the former regime to which Octavian owed his entire claim to leadership.

Any observer of the Roman political scene would have realized that radical changes were brewing, but few could have predicted the actual turn of events. Among the seeming possibilities would have been the dominance of Antony, a kind of interregnum, perhaps, while Octavian awaited his legitimate turn—at the age of twenty-seven, already prominently placed, Octavian could have afforded to wait. Or some sort of consular division of the expanding empire might have been expected to endure, with Antony responsible for the East and Octavian commanding the West. That this arrangement would prevail seemed indicated by the power compromises effected, first in the Pact of Brundisium in 40 B.C., and again three years later in the meeting at Tarentum (which Virgil himself may have attended). But quite soon the rivalry between the two men intensified, and Antony began to find himself at a serious disadvantage in the East while Octavian was building up power and winning "victories" on the Italian mainland.

From 36 to 32 B.C. Octavian saw a road to supreme power opening before him. Without crossing a single Rubicon, he moved forward determinedly, consolidating his positions, outmaneuvering Antony and offsetting the latter's successes, until eventually the Senate was prepared to give the young man full backing. Events swiftly moved toward the showdown at Actium. Modern scholars are still somewhat divided in their opinions as to the actual nature of this last act in the historical drama of the Roman Republic. Some argue that Plutarch romanticized the occasion and hold that Antony was in a fair way to win when, because of a series of flukes and false intelligence, all went against him. Others have followed the interpretations given by Roman writers bent on justifying Octavian's imperial mission and have viewed the triumph of Octavian as Roman retribution against an effete and lackluster Eastern spirit hostile to Rome and subversive of its best interests. Although we shall never recover the true story of what happened during those fateful days, there remains little doubt that they were critical in Roman history and of the utmost importance in shaping the Roman Empire of the future.

The decade surrounding the composition of the *Georgics* must have been a difficult and disturbed period for the Roman citizens who watched anxiously as their world pitched perilously on the high seas of historical change. How different that world would become they could hardly have surmised. Surely, the era must have appeared to them more like the preceding decades of a century beset with civil strife and partisan duels for power, with campaigns of foreign conquest, with appeals to the Senate to declare a state of emergency, with recurrent economic and social crises, than like a storm before the calm of imperial glory—the Pax Romana to be ushered in with the reign of Augustus (the title conferred on Octavian in 27 B.C.). Nevertheless, Virgil and his contemporaries were eyewitnesses to the "last revolution" in Roman history, and their hopes for the future, their conviction in the rightness of Roman ideals and Roman leadership, must have been sorely tried, challenged by some fundamental doubt as to whether any basis for the peaceful expansion of civilized life in the Western world would emerge from the chaotic struggles of the day. Even the perverse Antony was a different man, who baffled Cleopatra whenever, as Shakespeare put it, "a Roman thought . . . struck him."

This was the situation—a Roman world in the throes of violent change, Roman power fluctuating wildly, Roman loyalties divided, and Roman thoughts seriously endeavoring to solve the enigma of the future—that Virgil faced as he wrote the *Georgics*. At the request of Maecenas, the promising, thirty-four-year-old poet had undertaken a verse treatise on the subject of Roman farming. It was a tall order, as Virgil expressly remarked,[1] and it must have seemed a rather outlandish assignment, only remotely connected with the current crisis in Roman affairs. It required, for example, attention to things far different from the contest for power raging, dying out, flaring up again. Also, by the time Virgil, with characteristic deliberation and concern for the accuracy and fitness of his exposition, had spent seven years on his task and brought it to a conclusion, Octavian had become fully established in power. Hence

1. *Haud mollia iussa* (*Georgics* iii. 41).

in the *Georgics* we encounter various allusions to Octavian's eminence and references to him as embodying the hope of the future—the poet's hindsight creates the illusion of foresight.

On the other hand, it is little cause for wonder that we find Virgil recurring in the poem to thoughts of war and its implications, to preachments against it, to denunciations of its consequences. Virgil's attitude toward the cycle of aggression and counteraggression we soon come to recognize as not simply one of emotional horror. He is not simply against war. Rather, he seems to sense how fruitless the cycle becomes once it is entered upon, how one conflict leads to another just like it. No such one-sided expenditure of human energy, he wants to show us, can contribute anything useful or enduring to human life. And many images in the *Georgics* presented themselves to Virgil's mind as contrasts between the ways of war and the ways of peace: in every book of the *Georgics* references to war are made, sometimes dwelt upon. Over the whole work there glows a burnished contrast between the art of peace, whereby the indomitable farmer moves his curved plough through the earth, and the uncontrollable violence that would dispossess man of his rewards or distort the sanity of his behavior. Virgil takes notice, for example, of such things as the "war" of the elements, in the storm sequence of Book I, and the impact of civil war on Italy after Caesar's death, interrupting his exposition in mid-passage in the book and terminating it with a description of a world gone wild with fury, likened to a runaway chariot racing on frantically out of the driver's control. In Book II, given over for the most part to the calm subject of trees and vines, the poet delineates, though only in passing, the figure of Mars "in dubious battle," and at the end he gives vent to a caustic denunciation of "the Roman State, and empires doomed to die," levels his scorn at the frantic competitive pressures of "modern" life, and ends with a nostalgic allusion to bygone days before men had entered the iron age, the age of clashing weapons. In Book III, the battle of the bulls, the lurid description of animals at the mercy of unbridled sexual instincts, the temperamental, fiery warhorse contrasted with the majestically innocent ox, the Roman legionary on forced march, springing unexpectedly on his enemy—all these are among the contrasting elements that offset and complicate the farmer's mission. In Book IV we witness the miniature battle of the bees, see the rival "kings" fighting for control, and hear the reverberations of catastrophe when the king is lost or when the swarm succumbs to disease. Finally, in the eight-line epilogue, Virgil reminds us that he has been peacefully employed on his project, at leisure, while Octavian has been accumulating military victories in the East, winning his title to fame, paving the way for the future of Rome. The *Georgics* never entirely loses touch with the more sensational events of the day.

II. VIRGIL AND THE TRADITION

If Virgil's first problem was how to relate his poem to a world heaving with power politics and divisive feuds, the second problem was equally difficult. How could he compose an instructive poem full of facts and information about a technical subject without being merely dry, derivative, and dull? How, in fact, could one write something new about the oldest subject under the sun, earning a living from the soil?

As is characteristic of the classical poet, Virgil plunged boldly into the stream of a traditional literature. He would be like Hesiod, be the Roman Hesiod, sing Hesiod's song through Roman towns. We can, therefore, easily see the influence of Hesiod's *Works and Days* on Virgil's *Georgics*. Virgil meant us to see it, not to detect it by literary scholarship; for traditional things are those that civilization possesses in common, and Hesiod in this case would be the acknowledged predecessor. The Roman poet uses passages from the *Works and Days* and adapts lines from the earlier poem; he shares Hesiod's view of the necessity and respectability of manual labor. But, dependent as it is in certain fundamental ways upon the Greek model, Virgil's poem emerges as something totally different. We do not, in the end, recognize in Virgil's indomitable *agricola* Hesiod's dour and depressed *autourgos*. Whereas Hesiod had justified agriculture and indorsed it, bitterly enough at times, as a kind of technique for survival, Virgil glorified the subject and honored its prototype, the individual free farmer. Like Hesiod, Virgil saw that the farming life had its pains, but Virgil also saw that it clearly had its gains, and he took account of both sides. When one reads the *Georgics* alongside the *Works and Days*, it is remarkable how different Virgil's poem ultimately is. The *Georgics* is, to be sure, well seasoned with Hesiodic lore, sprinkled with re-workings and imitations of the Greek verses, illuminated on occasion by Hesiod's point of view. But in the end, and as a whole, the *Georgics* is nothing less than a total transformation of the traditional work on the subject.

The ability to work within a tradition and yet effect profound changes in it was, I believe, most marked in Virgil: his first work, the *Bucolics* (or *Eclogues*, as they are also known) was largely adapted from the tradition of Greek pastoral poetry, an "imitation" of Theocritus. Yet these ten "idyls" of Virgil formed a poetic master-piece unique in its own right, a new contribution to liter-ature. In his second work, the *Georgics*, Virgil reaches much farther back in the ancient tradition for a literary model and ends by having totally refashioned the geor-gic style. Ultimately, in the *Aeneid*, Virgil was to draw upon the original source of his literary tradition and pro-duce a masterful "imitation" of Homer that completely reoriented the epic style in Western literature.[2]

2. Later on, the lyric poet Horace was to observe, with typical aplomb, how Greece in her literature triumphed over her Roman mili-

"Georgics" is a transplanted Greek term for "the facts of farming," and for these Virgil would necessarily recur to the honored example of Boeotian Hesiod. But many more elements had become interwoven with the georgic tradition in antiquity by the time Virgil came to deal with it. Primarily, "didactic" poetry—the larger genus including all instructive verse, all art that teaches and informs—governed numerous species of literary product. Virgil himself studied many different sorts of didactic works, in verse and prose, emanating from sources as disparate as Theophrastus, Nicander of Colophon, Aratus, Varro, Lucretius. From youth he had been intellectually schooled in the Alexandrian tradition of erudite verse, which favored the sophisticated approach: the poet was expected to be widely informed, intelligent, resourceful in his art. And finally, among the specifically Roman contributions to his subject, Virgil studied old Cato's famous treatise, the *De agri cultura* (*ca.* 160 B.C.), and the fresh effort of Varro, the *De re rustica* (brought out in 37 B.C.). Merely to collate the various passages in the *Georgics* traceable to previous works in the tradition shows us how freely Virgil moved among the known authorities, choosing items of fact and interest

---

tary conquerors, and thus made Rome the literary captive of "Greek influence":

> Graecia capta ferum victorem cepit et artes
> intulit agresti Latio [*Epistles* ii. 1. 156–57].

But Virgil had already outwitted his friend and fellow poet by reversing the trend, by always improving upon the Greek original!

to incorporate into his own writing. The didactic tradition offered the poet many intrinsically valuable lessons, and he thus had a firm basis for the instructions he himself would formulate.

One other document confronting Virgil from the poetic tradition was Lucretius' verse essay, *On the Nature of Things*. Here was a work of art, daringly conceived and brilliantly executed, that Virgil could not disregard: the material itself was of first importance to anyone bent on studying natural processes and on discovering the operation of natural law. The noble grandeur of Lucretius' lines, the uncompromising rigor of his materialist doctrine, commanded Virgil's heartfelt respect. And for these very reasons, the precedent of Lucretius should have been a formidable barrier to Virgil in his attempt to continue along somewhat similar lines. Here again, however, as he had done with the focus on peace and tranquillity at a time of war and anxiety, Virgil converted the liability into an asset.

First of all, Virgil in his own poem occupied with applied science signified his firm recognition of Lucretius' concern with the whole problem of man's relation to nature. Among the best known lines of Virgil's poem are those expressing his celebrated "Homage to Lucretius":

> Felix qui potuit rerum cognoscere causas
> atque metus omnis et inexorabile fatum
> subiecit pedibus strepitumque Acherontis avari.

But, if we restore these lines to the complete context in which Virgil originally set them, we find that he has not merely assented to the inherited truth. Rather, he has added to it and so changed the idea and made it his own. He goes on immediately, for example, to add to this praise of his renowned precursor an equivalent praise, to be accorded to the man who, not entirely motivated to analyze nature, has chosen to appreciate nature's gifts and to appropriate them to his own uses. The passage in Book II of the *Georgics* opens, indeed, with Virgil's unfulfilled wish to penetrate scientifically into nature's secret workings. But it continues with his contented choice of the alternative satisfaction, living simply and appreciatively among the natural bounties of the good earth. There follow the lines hailing Lucretius' noble example, cited above, and finally the lines of equal importance:

> Fortunatus et ille deos qui novit agrestis,
> Panaque Silvanumque senem Nymphasque sorores.

The complete context, furthermore, the praise of country life terminating Book II, fully emphasizes the alternative way, not the scientific unmasking, but the intuitive enfolding of the mystery.

Is not Virgil's consistent attitude of reverence for nature, like his explicit reference to the very gods Lucretius had long since exiled, something of an affront to his mighty Roman forerunner? Confirmation of this opinion may be seen in another passage in the *Georgics* where Virgil deliberately sets about "imitating" Lucretius, with surprising results. Lucretius had written fervently of the typically Epicurean pleasure: watching, from a safe vantage point on shore, a storm-tossed ship floundering in the depths. Virgil describes an unlucky farmer who observes from a distance his lucky neighbor's towering grain heap, while he himself has been reduced to a starvation diet. In writing the lines, Virgil copied Lucretius' phrasing in the image just mentioned.[3] Most readers, Virgil knew, would spot the imitation, and relish it; but Virgil's inversion of the source signifies something more than mere poetic wit.

Has he not, if we consider the *Georgics* as a whole alongside the *De rerum natura* as a whole, consistently turned this item in the tradition inside out? Is not Virgil's poem by way of being a refutation of the materialist position, of the view that exalts pure science to the loftiest heights? The whole didactic tradition contained abundant materials for analyzing nature, for ransacking her secrets. Lucretius himself had pressed on his reader with the atomic realities and had argued in positively

3. Cf. *De rerum natura* ii. 1–2:

> Suave, mari magno turbantibus aequora ventis,
> e terra magnum alterius spectare laborem;
> non quia vexari quemquamst iucunda voluptas,
> sed quibus ipse malis careas quia cernere suave est

with *Georgics* i. 158–59:

> heu magnum alterius frustra spectabis acervum,
> concussaque famem in silvis solabere quercu.

cosmic dimensions that man was the reasoning atom, adrift among the nature of things, buoyed up by intelligence alone, a material object himself, albeit of the most refined sort.

Virgil recognized the value of this approach; he absorbed the necessary information and applied it where necessary.[4] But he refused to let the point of view dominate him, for it could not and did not encompass the full description of man. Where Lucretius' interest had led him to the nature of things, to man's subordination in the material universe, Virgil's led him to the things of nature, to the purpose, duty, and powers of man, to the centrality of man in the whole scheme. Virgil's *agricola* must know about nature, but more than that he must do something about her, apply himself and so master the material. The hardworking, canny countryman (*acer rusticus*), the irritated ploughman (*iratus arator*), the painstaking shepherd—all these figures combine to shape the image of a supremely respectable type of human behavior, the dignified pursuit of work and its rewards. Science and its practical application form an important part of man's heritage. But conscience, motive, and purposeful accomplishment also form an important part of our lives.

It is by studying the career, as it were, of the anonymous farmer that Virgil both acknowledges and liber-

4. Lucretius would surely have relished Virgil's no-nonsense analysis of the changing temperaments of birds (*Georgics* i. 410 ff.).

ates himself from the influence of Lucretius. The topical situation had challenged the poet's power to develop a positive image of peace and productiveness. The literary and scientific tradition had required his attention to the facts and submitted at least one major model for his imagination to cope with. But above all, the "didactic" tradition still left something for Virgil to teach, something new and positive to say. He would instruct his world in the art of applied science, in the right exercise of a technique, set within the larger framework of scientific fact and natural law. He would reveal the dynamic spiritual forces motivating the application of human effort.

III. THE "GEORGICS" AS A WORK OF ART

Turning to the poem itself, we notice that Virgil has chosen a somewhat unusual structure for the *Georgics*. He deals in Book I with the soil, its qualities and its problems, with ploughing, sowing and harvesting, and the weather. In Book II he proceeds directly to the culture of trees, to the landscape with its familiar vineyards and olive groves. He also discusses in this book many varieties of forest stand and of shrubs, and he considers various uses of lumber. Book III deals with animals, the cattle, horses, sheep, and goats, looking now, as it were, at the beings that people the land and roam over the landscape.

The farm animals also impose on their keeper a variety of duties, as stock-breeder, trainer, and veterinarian, adept in pastoral care. Book IV divides into two main parts, the first a description and natural history of the honeybees, the second a mythical narrative telling how Aristaeus, "the first beekeeper," discovered the technique for regenerating a swarm.

External parallels in structure contribute an evident balance to the whole exposition: the fury of civil war at the end of Book I, for example, clearly matches the furious onslaught of the plague at the end of Book III; the serene eulogies in Book II, first of Italy and then of country life in general, match the Corycian idyl of Book IV and the "happy ending" of the same book. The reader will of course find numerous instances of parallelism and contrast, and of variation and balance, and will note subtle effects of verbal reminiscence and thematic counterpoint that all go to reinforce the unity of Virgil's four-part and four-square almanac. I think, however, that the unity of the *Georgics* is not to be identified with the careful calculations of the poetic mind: the rhetorical arrangement is obviously a clue, but in itself it does not reveal the unity of conception which endows the work with its total power to evoke aesthetic appreciation. Today, in fact, for the modern taste not schooled in the discipline of oral poetry, of a recitation modulated to the ear and attuned to the rather physiological faculty of "attention," much in the structure of the *Georgics* may seem difficult. For example, transitions are seldom spelled out: one must feel rather than see how the links join. Abrupt changeovers from one detail to another, from one subject to the next, come upon us quite swiftly as we read the printed page. The four books follow boldly upon one another without regard for devices of repetition or summarizing. No review of the subject matter at regular intervals comes to aid the reader's digestion of it.

Virgil has given us, instead of rhetoric, a dramatic vision of life and labor on the land. Combining floridity of detail with grandeur of description, rigorous doctrine with inspired convictions, exposure to the whole subject with saturation in four aspects of it (which well describe its general boundaries), he has imagined what he thinks the reader ought to know. The *Georgics* is Virgil's "field." Its methodical instructions, its contours, and its depths as Virgil paints them in, its creatures and their behavior, its vignettes and genre scenes, its cautions and its counsels, the modulations of tone, the anecdotes, epigrams, the fable—all these constitute the imperial province of Virgil's poetic mind.

The author is forever after us with the facts. Things like crop-rotation, irrigation, clearing arable land, grafting and pruning, spacing the vines and olives, selecting their sites, must be stated in shrewd, practical terms. The farmer is a cattle-raiser, too, and his own dairyman. He may want to go in for something special, like honey, and cannot afford to get stung in the process. All of this we must see, and see clearly. It is disenchanting to a degree to realize how even today, sheer manual method figures in the farmer's program. But the man's knowledge must still come out at his fingertips. Even the beekeeper, Virgil reminds us, must expect to "wear out his hands with hard work."[5]

But Virgil's efforts enable us to do more than see what goes on; they enable us to see into the life of things, to envisage and appreciate the conception motivating the farmer's daily round. The *agricola* goes through a cycle of productive labor:

> ... redit agricolis labor actus in orbem
> atque in se sua per vestigia volvitur annus.[6]

And as he works through his schedule, diversely occupied, now with the soil, now with the forest land and fruit trees, now with the livestock, now with his special item of production, he moves nearer and nearer the good life. The farmer's essential pleasure lies in this "circle" of duty, the performance of work made familiar and manageable by its renewal. He enjoys the incomparable satisfaction of playing a unique role in an age-old but ageless setting.

The good earth can easily enough turn into the bad

5. *Ibid.* iv. 114: *ipse labore manum duro terat.*
6. *Ibid.* ii. 401–2:
    The farmers' work returns to them full circle—
    Their year revolves, retracing its own steps.

earth. We see Virgil's farmer up against it at times, reeling under the blows of nature as he fights back against disease, blight, pests, frost and heat waves, drought or flood, and scans the heavens for clues to the weather, *varium et mutabile semper*. We also, however, see the farmer in command of the situation more often than not, slicing a fine furrow in the life-bearing earth, fashioning and shaping the fruit trees to promote a superior growth, nursing along his animals attentively, breaking them into their work, tending them at foaltime, shielding them from disease and snakes. At the end, the bees, those flower-farmers, work for the keeper, who now stands at one remove from the scene of labor and reaps his sweet reward. Here is progress, plain and homespun perhaps, but real and tangible.

Another form of progress the farmer knows is the spiritual satisfaction of counting his blessings. At the end of Book II Virgil eloquently enumerates these familiar items, peace and rest after struggle and work, abundance of harvest, well-stocked barns, a frolicsome family and a host of cheerful friends, success recollected in tranquillity. These things and many more like them comprise Virgil's dramatic unfolding of man in action, the child of nature, the master of his environment.

Readers who return to the Latin text from a translation of the *Georgics* will rediscover how unique the embodiment of this ideal has become in Virgil's hands. English translators in particular, from Dryden to the present, have ever acknowledged the superiority of Virgil's faultless phrasing, of his dexterous, felicitous rhythms, of the fugal continuity of image, idea, and statement. A translation can only point the way to Virgil's lines, for what Virgil uniquely imagined cannot be duplicated. Every man must see it his own way, in his own light, illuminated by Virgil's vision.

The *Georgics* has consistently appealed to men of all sorts and conditions. Medieval literature shows definite traces of its influence. Renaissance and seventeenth-century writers knew it as part of their stock in trade Eighteenth-century English literature, in particular exalted the vogue of the *Georgics* to its height, and Virgil's poem provided the main impulse for a new kind of landscape poetry that would rival the Latin source. Today, I believe, the poetry of Robert Frost, with its canny pastoral realism and inspired wit, is akin to Virgil's spirit in the *Georgics*. Or again, the example of the late Louis Bromfield, in his life and his work evangelically bent on recording his love for the land, reminds us that Virgil's kind of mentality is far from obsolete. Or again, T. S. Eliot has found time to voice his assent with the actual:

> And right action is freedom
> From past and future also.
> For most of us, this is the aim
> Never here to be realized;
> Who are only undefeated
> Because we have gone on trying;
> We, content at the last

If our temporal reversion nourish
(Not too far from the yew tree)
The life of significant soil.[7]

The final victory of the *Georgics* belongs more properly to art than to agriculture. A good part of Virgil's subject is now outdated, and many of his facts mere museum pieces. The genuine miracle is that from a prosaic and plain subject matter Virgil is still capable of bringing new life, new interest, new understanding to the reader. And this miracle is simply the result of one aesthetic fact—the generation of life through words. Everything comes alive when Virgil writes about it: the trees "feel" and "have character," the south wind "plans" to act up, the plants "lift up their hearts," the crops "rejoice," the ploughland is, on occasion, "mournful." The reader of the *Georgics* sees, now close-up, now in noble panorama, the land and the landscape and feels the presence of nature in her various moods. Patterns of behavior are depicted in the animals: the guileless ox, the belligerent bull, the flashing horse, capricious goats and compliant sheep, the vengeful, creepy serpent, land and sea birds darting and soaring over the scene, the crafty ant, "exiguous" mouse, talkative frogs. In the bees Virgil foreshadows a Fabre or Maeterlinck in psychological finesse while he harks back to the moral delight of an Aesop.

Instructive as his bees are, however, Virgil records

7. *Four Quartets*, "The Dry Salvages."

that their behavior lacks freedom: for this group, *drive* is identical with *will*. For the Roman reader, the point must have been rather delicious. After all, the most marked attribute of the Roman genius was its superlative will power: fighters and subduers, lawmakers and law-givers, engineers, builders, planners, performers—the long line of practical Romans did not exactly have power thrust upon them. Rather, these people struggled to gain the leadership of their world, deliberately planning and carrying out what they considered to be the right way of life. Now, when we study Virgil's bees, who, as the poet says, "serve their king more slavishly than Persians/Than Parthia's people, or Egypt's"[8] we learn something about the peril of this efficiently lubricated "one-man" rule. Their high degree of organization makes us appreciate the maximum of order, but their enslavement to their own system gives us pause. The tightly organized economic unit, for instance, always runs the risk of disintegration *as a whole:* the unit is the swarm. The leader has become too indispensable.

For the other side of the picture, witness the end of the *Georgics*, the last half of the last book. Scholars have sometimes referred to this section as unsatisfactory, in-harmonious with, or too different from, the rest. But let us ask ourselves why Virgil of his own free will chose to end by telling his reader a story. The narrative is, by turns, enchanting, surrealistic, weird, and enigmatic,

8. *Georgics* iv. 210–12.

moving, somber. It proceeds through disheartening reversals of situation to the ultimate phenomenon of regeneration. Aristaeus, mythical prototype of the farmer as keeper and caretaker, has lost his swarm. Virgil has already shown us, in the first half of this book, how a swarm can go to pieces. Immured in their own system, the bees cannot be saved except by recourse to some such thing as regeneration, and hence the pure, if persistent, fiction of the regeneration-technique. The technique itself being erroneous, we are entitled to assume that Virgil was working at this point in his poem, *non verissime sed decentissime* (as Seneca put it). My opinion is that Virgil was now more interested in the idea and the inference of his fiction than in its factual relevance.

For what the story tells us is that Aristaeus "misbehaved." The hero, having lost control of himself, had lost his swarm and had lost his touch. Inadvertently provoking the death of Eurydice, Aristaeus was suffering the wrath of Orpheus when he descended into the watery environment of his mother's realm. Cyrene thereupon led him to Proteus, who, overpowered, told Aristaeus the story of Orpheus and Eurydice. What Orpheus' effort to regain Eurydice signifies is, of course, the spectacle of an energy expended (on behalf of another) to recover and foster human life. But Aristaeus simply heard the story as Proteus told it to him, and thereupon was informed of how to placate the shades of Orpheus and Eurydice by means of a ritual technique resulting in regeneration of his swarm of bees. In the last lines, the productive energy delineated throughout the poem bursts out once more, as from the corpses of cattle laid in the ground a new swarm of bees soars aloft to hang from the boughs of a nearby tree like a cluster of grapes.

Surely, Virgil has not just tacked on this ending to spruce up the poem and enliven a dull subject. The *Georgics* is alive from the very first word, and here, with a grace beyond the reach of art, Virgil has wrought his climax. Book IV first studies the group, a society at the height of efficient production, for all that that implies. It then studies individuals, unique in any society, whose purposeful efforts can alone, in the end, keep society operating, nurture its life, and shape its future. Orpheus is traditionally a figure associated with agriculture as the life-bearing, peaceful, and civilizing venture. He is the enemy of hostility, the patron of humanity. Virgil's Orpheus (seen in the *Georgics*, incidentally, for the first time at full-length in the literature of antiquity now extant) becomes the heroic image of man's will to preserve life.

Life cannot be regenerated. Virgil knew that as well as we do. Virgil has, however, avowed at several points in his previous exposition his explicit intention to do something new with the honored and dignified tradition of instructive verse. Perhaps by the time he had arrived at the middle of Book IV, he felt that he had been quite educational enough, that it was time for the reader to be entertained, to be awarded some opportunity for leisure and reflection after the unflagging indoctrination of a most practical poem. I think he did in fact so innovate and in so doing imparted his own spirit as man and artist to the work he had undertaken. It is not, ultimately, regeneration that is at stake in the *Georgics*. It is not sheer method, the ceaseless round of work, the rivers of sweat, that command our final respect. It is, rather, the whole life displayed here, the work and the plan, the reward and the results. The farmer's life is even more appreciable than his skill.

As Keats serenely expressed it, "The poetry of earth is never dead." Virgil shows us the living poetry. He impresses it on our minds, and in his art the truth is made incarnate. Virgil's hero is a hardy *agricola*, animated by his very belief in life, impelled by his appreciation of the earth's bounty, governed by intelligence, inspired by purpose. Before our eyes, the farmer re-enacts the profound experience of man, the master of his environment, ruler of the variegated life that surrounds him. He is neither the slave of subsistence nor the animal that survives by struggling instinctively. Voluntarily, and with a genuinely Roman glory, he blazes the trail to abundance, confident that his efforts will enable himself and his fellow men to live well and to live on.

SMITH PALMER BOVIE

BARNARD COLLEGE
June 1, 1956

BOOK ONE

What makes the crops rejoice, beneath what star
To plough, and when to wed the vines to elms,
The care of cattle, how to rear a flock,
How much experience thrifty bees require:
Of these, Maecenas, I begin to sing.
You, sun and moon, our world's resplendent lights,
Who lead the year revolving through the skies;
And Bacchus and kind Ceres, by whose grace
Earth exchanged acorns for fertile grain
And mingled rivers' waters with new wine;
You, Fauns, the country's ever-present spirits,
(Come, oh Fauns, and dance with the Dryad maids!):
Your gifts I sing. And Neptune, whose great fork
Struck earth and first produced the neighing steeds;
And Aristaeus, guardian of groves,
Whose herds in hundreds graze Aegean lands;
And Pan, good shepherd, leave your native groves
And vales, to bless us in Arcadia here;
Come, Minerva, patron of the olive,
Triptolemus, the hero of the plough,

Silvanus with a young and slender cypress:
All gods and goddesses who guard the fields,
Protecting random fruit and showering rain
On seedling plants: be with us now.
You also we would hail, oh godlike man,
Octavian Caesar: you will be a god,
But in what form the gods do not reveal;
You may become a deity of land
Protecting towns and fields, a great provider,
Lord of seasons, crowned with Venus' myrtle
Whom the mighty sphere of earth receives;
You may come as a god of boundless ocean
Whom distant shores and sailors worship solely
And Mother Ocean seeks for her own daughter;
You may find place among the constellations,
Linked to summer's chain of lazy months
There, between the Scorpion and Virgo—
The Scorpion contracts to leave you room—
Whatever form you take, O Caesar, never
Will the underworld have hope of you as king,
For no such crude desire for domination
Possesses you, although the Greeks adore
Elysian fields, and Proserpine recalled
Has no desire to stay beside her mother:
Whatever form, O Caesar, you assume,

Smooth my path, condone this enterprise
Of bold experiment in verse, and share
Concern with me for uninstructed farmers:
Grow used to prayers appealing to your name.

When Spring is new, and frozen moisture thaws
On white-clothed mountainsides, and crumbling soil
Is loosened by the West Wind, let your bull
Begin to groan beneath the pressing plough
And the well-worn ploughshare gleam from the rub of
    the furrow.
The crop alone that twice has felt the sun,
And twice the cold, hears greedy farmers' prayers,
And its heavy harvests often burst a barn.
But before we plough an unfamiliar patch
It is well to be informed about the winds,
About the variations in the sky,
The native traits and habits of the place,
What each locale permits, and what denies.
One place is good for crops, one happier
With grapes; in other places orchards bloom,
Or grasses flourish freely. You have seen
How Lydia sends us saffron for perfume,
How India sends us ivory; frankincense
Comes from the soft Sabaeans; naked tribes
Of the Chalybes give iron, and Pontus yields

Pungent musk; Epirus nurtures mares
That win the Olympics. Nature made these laws
These everlasting pacts, at just the time
Deucalion cast the stones on the empty sphere
And a hardy race of men sprang up. So come,
And let your strong bulls overturn rich soil
With the first months of the year, let dusty heat
Bake through the upturned clods with ripening suns;
But if the earth is barren, it will suit
To raise a lightly hanging furrow ridge
When Arcturus rises: do the former,
That the weeds may not obstruct prolific crops,
The latter, that the slender thread of damp
May not drain off and leave a desert waste.

In alternation let the new-cut fields
Lie fallow so the untouched plain crusts over,
Lying idle; or when the seasons shift
Sow in golden grain where previously
You raised a crop of beans that gaily shook
Within their pods, or a tiny brood of vetch,
Or the slender stems and rustling undergrowth
Of bitter lupine. Crops of flax burn out
A field, oats burn it through, and drowsy poppies
Soaked in oblivious sleep will burn it too:
But still, rotation makes your labor easy,

As long as you are not ashamed to drench
The arid soil with fertile dung, and scatter
Grimy ashes through the worn-out land.
Thus will the land find rest in its change of crop,
And earth left unploughed show you gratitude.
Set sterile lands on fire; it turns out well
To scorch the empty stalks with crackling flames;
From this the land conceives a secret strength
And fertile sustenance; or all defect
Melts off, and useless moisture sweats away;
Or heat thereby expands the many ducts
And hidden pores through which the juice may reach
New grass; or, heat may stiffen up the earth,
Contract the gaping veins, offset the thrust
Of freezing North winds, counter fine-spun rain
And the too intensive force of blazing suns.
The man who breaks the sluggish clods apart
With his hoe, and drags his wicker harrow through
Delights the land, and golden-yellow Ceres
Watches him with pride from high Olympus;
He also serves who, having raised the ridges
Cutting through the plain, turns round his plough
And breaks them through on horizontal lines,
Who drills the earth and takes command of the field.
   Pray for wet midsummers, farmer friends,

And clear, cold winter skies; with the winter's dust
The fields are glad, the grain is overjoyed.
Nothing else so puffs up Mysia's pride,
Or makes Mount Gargara marvel at its yield.
Need I mention him who scatters seed,
Then closes with the soil, his hoe in hand,
And smooths the barren ridges flat, and then
Guides toward the crops the channels of a stream,
And when the scorched earth swelters, and its grass
Is moribund, taps water from the brow
Of the hillside stream? This water, rippling down
Past smooth-worn stones, gives rise to rough-voiced
    murmurs,
And its gushing currents temper thirsty fields.
Need I tell of him who grazes down
Luxuriance in early blades of corn
As soon as the crops draw level with the furrow,
That the stalk be not weighed down with heavy ears?
Of him who drains the swamps' collected damp
Away from the soaked light earth? In doubtful months
Especially, when swollen rivers rise
And silt up mud that binds the whole locale
And sends off tepid mist from hollow pools.

  Nor yet, though men and oxen have so long
Laboriously turned the soil, do impudent geese

And cranes desist from mischief, shade of trees
Do no harm, sharp endive cease to obstruct.
⟋ The Father willed it so: He made the path
Of agriculture rough, established arts
Of husbandry to sharpen human wits,
Forbidding sloth to settle on his soil.
Before Jove, farms and farmers were unknown;
To mark off or divide the land was wrong,
For things were held in common, and the earth
Brought forth her substance then, more generously,
When none imposed demands upon the ground.
Jove endowed the serpents with their venom,
Commanded wolves to prowl and seas to rise,
Shook honey from the leaves, hid fire away,
Stopped up the streams of wine, so that mankind
By taking thought might learn to forge its arts
From practice: seek to bring the grain from furrows,
Strike out the fire locked up in veins of flint.
Then rivers first bore hollow boats, and sailors
Numbered the stars and named them: Pleiades,
The Hyades, the radiant Northern Bear.
Men discovered how to trap and hunt,
How to circle forests with their hounds;
Some plunged their casting nets deep in broad rivers,
While others trailed their dripping lines at sea.

Harsh iron emerged, and saws with whistling blades
(For earlier, men split their logs with wedges);
Then followed all the civilizing arts:
Hard labor conquered all, and pinching need.

   Ceres first taught men to plough the land,
When acorns and arbutus disappeared;
But soon enough the wheat fields came to grief:
A mildew blight fell on the golden stems,
The lazy thistle flourished in the fields,
The crops went under, and a wood of brambles,
Goose-grass, and star-thistles took their place.
Unlucky darnel and wild oats held sway
Among the gleaming rows. Unless your hoe
Attacks the weeds unceasingly, unless
You chase off thieving birds with frightful shouts,
And prune away the shady darkening growth,
Unless you pray for rain, in helpless want
You'll gaze upon a neighbor's teeming store
And soothe your hunger pangs with forest acorns.

   Now I must describe the armaments
Tough country-dwellers use, without which crops
Could not be sown nor raised; the ploughshare, first,
And the curved plough's heavy stock. Demeter's slow-
   wheeled
Carts, remorseless heavy hoes, the harrows,

Threshing tables; also, wicker ware
Of the common sort that Celeus used, and hurdles
Of arbutus wood, and Iacchus' ritual fans.
All these things you provide for in advance
If you would earn the country's sacred praise.
The elm, still in the forest, bent by might,
 As a plough-tail, will assume the plough's curved shape.
To its stock are fixed two mold-boards, an eight-foot
    pole,
And the share-beam's double back. A limber lime
Is felled in advance for the yoke, and a lofty beech
Selected for the handle that will turn
The undercarriage from behind; the wood
Then hangs above the hearth for the smoke to cure.

    I now pass on to you some old advice,
Unless you shrink back, loath to learn slight points.
Above all, level off the threshing floor
With a heavy roller, knead it down by hand
And bind it well with chalk to kill the weeds
And keep the crumbling dust from opening chinks:
For then all sorts of plagues will pester you:
Often underground the scanty mouse
Sets up his homes and builds his granaries,
Or moles deprived of sight dig out their room;
The toad is found in holes, and countless pests

That lands support; the weevil ravages
A mighty heap of grain, as does the ant
On guard against a lean old age. Observe, too,
When the almond tree that grows so thick in forests
Puts on her blossoms, curves her fragrant boughs:
If the fruit abounds, abundant crops ensue,
And heavy threshing comes, intense with heat;
If shade predominates, with wealth of leaf,
Your floor will thresh stalks only rich in chaff.
Many sowers treat their seeds ahead,
I notice, soak with solvent alkali
And black oil-lees, so the tricky pods may yield
A larger crop, and when put on to boil,
Cook fast and well, however slight the flame.
I've often noticed, too, that seeds go bad
Though sorted and inspected carefully,
Unless the human effort, year by year,
Picks out the best by hand. So fate requires
That all things whirl to ruin, slip behind,
Like one who rows his skiff against the current,
Touch and go: if once his arms ease off,
The current sweeps him headlong down the stream.

   We need to watch the stars, Arcturus' phase,
The Kids', the bright Snake, just as sailors do
Who beat down windswept Pontus, homeward bound,

Or brave the jaws of Mysia's oyster straits.
When Libra brings in balance day and night,
Bisects our world in halves of light and shade,
Then work your oxen, sow your barley, men,
To the very verge of stubborn rainswept winter.
The time is here for cover crops of flax
And Ceres' poppy, time for wielding ploughs
While dried-out earth permits and clouds hang high.
The time for beans is Spring; the crumbling furrows
Welcome you, lucerne with length of life,
And millet makes its annual demands
When snow-white Taurus' gilded horns disclose
The coming year, and Canis fades away
From his rival star. But if you work the ground
To harvest wheat or sturdy spelt, and count
On grain alone, before you plant the seeds
The furrows lack, and hurry out to trust
Your whole year's hope to reluctant earth, the Dawn
Should find the morning Pleiads stealing off
And Ariadne's fiery crown withdrawn.
Many start before the Pleiad sets,
But with worthless oats the long-expected crop
Eludes them. If you sow the homely bean
Or vetch, and deign to grow Egyptian lentils,
Boötes in decline will furnish you

Clear-sighted indications. So, begin
And stretch your sowing out halfway through frosts.
  For the golden Sun commands his sphere, marked
    off
In fixed divisions through the Zodiac.
Five zones bind the heavens: one of these
Glows fiery red with the everlasting sun;
Around this zone at either end, two more
Extend dark-hued to right and left, transfixed
In ice and pitch-black storms; within these three,
The frigid zones and torrid center, two
Have been conceded mortals by the gods,
Allowing for our frailty: a path
Divides them both, whereon the angled line
Of tandem constellations may revolve.
As our world rises steeply toward the heights
Of Russia, so it slopes back down again
To press on Libya's southland. Over us
The one pole veers aloft, the one below
Appears to murky Styx and sunken ghosts.
Above, the sinuous Snake unwinds his coils,
Flows river-like between the double Bears
That dread to plunge in Ocean's wave. Below,
They say, eternal night lies hushed and calm,
That shadows roll up thick beneath night's cloak,

Or Dawn returns our day to them; when here
The orient's breathless steeds requicken us,
Out there the glowing Dusk lights evening's rays.
In doubtful skies we can, therefore, predict
A weather change, the time to sow and reap,
The time to lash the treacherous calm with oars,
To launch rigged ships, fell forest-seasoned pines:
And not in vain we scan the rise and fall
Of star-led signs, the balanced four-part year.
    When cold rain keeps him in, the farmer can
Get on with some work, at ease, he would have to rush
If the sky were clear; the ploughman batters straight
His blunted share's hard edge, or hollows troughs
From logs, or brands his herd, or tags his heaps.
Others sharpen stakes or two-pronged forks,
Or fashion Umbrian willow bands to hold
Their limber vines. Now lace your Rubine boughs
In pliant baskets, dry and grind your corn
By fire and stone. For even holidays
Within our law and scruples we are free
To carry on some work; no holy law
Forbids our clearing ditches, shielding crops
With hedges, setting bird snares, burning thorns
And plunging bleating flocks in healthful streams.
A driver loads his lazy donkey's sides

With oil or low-grade fruits, and brings from town
A rough millstone or massive lump of pitch.

   The moon herself has organized the days
In various sequence prosperous for work.
Avoid the fifth, pale Orcus' and the Furies'
Natal day; when Earth in ghastly labor
Bore Iapetus and Coeus, wild Typhoeus,
And the brothers sworn to break their way into heaven.
They tried three times, in fact, to heave up Ossa
On Pelion, and to roll leaf-clad Olympus
Up on Ossa. Three times, father Jove
Reft the mountainous pile with his thunderbolt.
The seventeenth bodes well for planting vines,
For breaking oxen, yoking them, and tying
Leashes to your warp. The ninth bodes well
For runaways, is hostile to the thief.

   Much is better done at chilly night,
Or when the morning star diffuses dew
On earth at dawn. It's best to cut
At night the weightless stubble, dried-out fields:
For softening moisture never fails at night.
Beside the winter firelight's evening blaze
One farmer stays awake and splits up wood
For torches with his knife. And all the while
His wife relieves her lengthy task with song,

And runs the squeaky shuttle through the warp,
Or boils down sweetened wine-must over flame,
And skims with leaves the bubbling cauldron's wave.
But Ceres' ruddy grain is best cut down
In midday heat, in midday heat the floor
Best threshes dried-out corn. So, strip to plough
And strip to sow; for wintertime means ease
To husbandmen. Most farmers will enjoy
Their gains in cold spells, keeping company,
And enjoy themselves. For Winter, cheerful host,
Invites them in and thaws out all their cares;
Like sailors when the laden keels reach port
Who joyfully wreathe their garlands on the stern.
But still, now is the time to strip the olives,
Acorns, laurel-berries, blood-red myrtle,
To set out snares for cranes and traps for deer,
And course the long-eared hare, and shoot the roe,
Whirling slings with thongs of Spanish hemp,
When snow lies deep, when rivers pile up ice.

Why tell the Autumn's tempests and her stars
When days are shortened, summer mollified,
And men must be on guard? Need I describe
The rush of Spring, rain-laden, on the fields
Of bristling grain and stems of milky corn?
Often I have seen the battling winds

Tear a heavy crop up by the roots,
And toss it far and wide, just as the farmer
Led his mowers in to strip the barley:
The tempest, in a black and twisting cloud,
Swept away the blade and flying chaff.
For often rain forms mighty battle lines
And clouds collect aloft, to pile on high
A murky storm: the high sky crashes down,
Rains flood the happy fields our oxen worked;
Ditches swell and the hollow streams expand,
Ocean seethes and moans in her narrow fiords.
In the storm cloud's midnight, Jove himself wields fire
In his flashing fist, the mighty earth recoils
With the shock, and panic puts the beasts to flight,
While crouching terror levels human hearts.
With sizzling bolt he strikes down Rhodopé,
Scores Athos, rends the Acroceraunian Cape.
The wind redoubles, rain intensifies,
As woods and shore moan with the screeching blast.
So, take precautions, learn the months and seasons,
Mark chilly Saturn's course, watch Mercury
On his flaming rounds; and venerate the gods,
Performing Ceres' rites upon the grass
At Autumn's close and in the sunlit Spring.
The lambs are fattest then, and wine most mellow,

Sleep is sweet; the shade lies thick on hillsides.
See that your country folk adore the goddess:
For her let milk and honey flow, and wine,
And lead the sacrificial victims round the crops
Three times, to bring good fortune, let a chorus
Follow the procession, singing hymns
To Ceres, ask her blessing on their homes;
Let no one lay his sickle to the grain
Until, with festive oak wreath on his brow,
He honors Ceres' name in dance and song.
   To teach us by sure signs when to expect
Heat waves, storms, the driving cold of winds,
The Father himself decreed what the monthly moon
Should tell us; under what star the South Wind drops;
Repeatedly, when to keep the herds near their stalls.
For when the wind is rising, ocean straits
Heave restlessly, a dry and crackling sound
Is heard on mountain heights, the shores resound
With mingling echoes, forest murmurs swell;
The wave frets nervously at the vessel's keel,
And gulls fly swiftly in from sea to land,
Screaming on the shore, and scavengers
Dart dizzily above the barren sand;
The heron leaves his marsh to soar on high.
Impending wind will show you shooting stars

That slip from the sky and glide across the dusk,
Their long wake incandescent in the night;
Upflying leaves and chaff will catch your eye,
Or feathers dancing on the water's crest.
But when it lightens from the hostile North,
Or thunder rolls in from the East and West,
The rural lands will flood, the ditches fill,
And sailors furl their damp sails out at sea.
Rain never need surprise us unprepared,
For when it rises, airborne cranes take off,
And glide along the valley floor, or a heifer
Glances up and sniffs with flaring nostrils,
Or twittering swallows flit across the lake,
And frogs, in the mud, croak out their ancient objec-
    tions.
The ant brings out her eggs from hiding places
Deep in the earth, and makes her narrow path;
A rainbow's mighty arc sucks at the ground,
A group of crows, arrayed in line, deserts
The feeding ground to creak in flight formation.
Then birds flock in, of every sort, like those
That play along the meadows of the East
Near Ionia's still, fresh-water pools:
They outdo one another sprinkling spray
Across their shoulders, then they plunge in deep,

Or skim the waves and take sheer joy in bathing.
The raven calls for rain, that wretched bird
Who, croaking hoarsely, stalks along the sand
In solitary splendor. And even maidens,
Spinning at their looms, can sense the storm,
When oil starts sputtering in the burning lamp
And a moldy fungus gathers on the wick.

When rain is past, you may discern as well
And recognize by surest indications
Clear and sunny days. The stars' bright edge
Is sharply outlined then, the moon comes up
Without assistance from her brother's rays,
No lacy clouds of wool drift through the sky;
Not now will Thetis' favored halcyons
Spread forth their wings to catch the warming sun
On shoreline, nor the messy pigs take thought
To root and nose about in heaps of straw.
The mists prefer to find low ground and hang
Down on the plain, the night owl keeps a watch
On sunset from a high perch, and aimlessly
Spins out her evening song. Then Nisus shines
On high in the pure clear air, as Scylla pays
For the crimson lock she stole: her feathers slice
Through space, but where she flees, King Nisus whirs
In hot pursuit; he mounts: her feathers slice

Through space in panic. Now you will hear the crows
Chanting their soft refrains from narrow throats
And chattering high in the leaves from lofty nests,
Beside themselves with some exceptional joy;
The rain gone, they delight to see their fledglings
And their cozy nests again; not from divine
Intelligence, I think, nor that Fate endows
The birds with foresight, but that simply when
The weather and fitful vapors change their course,
When Jove's wet South breath thickens up the rare,
Or clears again, and rarefies the dense,
The birds' hearts feel these moves: they change their
    minds,
And adapt themselves to motions now distinct
From those they felt when the wind drove on the
    clouds.
This cause accounts for field birds' harmony,
For happy herds, for the throaty cheers of crows.
    If you observe the fiery sun, and moon
In systematic phase, tomorrow's hour
Will never fool you, nor will tranquil night
Enmesh you in her snares. For if, when the moon
First gathers her returning fire, she grasps
Between both horns a field of misty dark,
For land and sea a heavy rain is in store;

If maiden blushes steal across her face
The wind will rise: when golden Phoebe reddens,
Wind is in store; and one infallible guide
Is the new moon, seen on the fourth day after her rising:
If then she glides through heaven with undimmed
   horns,
All clear; that day and all the rest of the month
Will miss the wind and rain; and safe on shore,
The sailors pay respects to Panopea,
To Glaucus and to Ino's favorite son.

   The sun, arising, settling in the waves,
Gives weather signs of surest consequence,
Which come with morning or the rising stars.
When hidden in a cloud he scatters spots
Across his budding dawn or shrinks away
From his center disk, look out for rain:
For then the South Wind whistles in from sea
Intent on wrecking trees and crops and herds.
Or when, at dawn, his scattered rays break through
Dense cloudbanks, when Aurora rises pale
To leave Tithonus' saffron marriage bed,
Ah, then the poor vine-leaf has no defense
For her tender grapes! Such brittle bursts of hail
Dance crackling over roofs. Observe well, too,
When, setting, he has measured off the sky;

We see a range of colors cross his face:
Dark hues declare for rain, and flaming red
For East winds. But if mingling spots appear
In his molten fire, you'll see all nature heave
With storm and wind: on such a night, no one
Convinces me to venture on the deep,
To cast off from the land. If his disk shines clear
When he restores or hides again our day,
You fear the clouds in vain and you shall see
That forest lands are swayed by clear North Wind.
In short, the sun will give you all the signs:
What promises the tardy dusk conveys,
From what direction wind drives tranquil clouds,
And what the dripping South Wind has in mind.
Does anyone dare say the sun is false?
He warns us when uprisings threaten blindly,
And furtive actions breed conspiracy.
He pitied Rome when Caesar was destroyed,
Concealed his radiant head in obscure gloom
And godless men feared everlasting night.
At that time, earth and sea, and baying hounds,
Uneasy birds, foreshadowed evil days.
How often we saw Aetna burst her bounds,
Hurling liquid rocks and fiery mass!
Germany heard weapons clash on high,

The Alps shook with a strange and fearful motion.
Uncanny voices sounded in the woods,
And ghastly phantom forms materialized.
The cattle uttered words (unspeakable!),
Streams stood still and chasms rent the earth;
Ivory statues wept, and bronze perspired.
The river Po swept through the woods with rage,
His maddened flood bore herds and barns away,
And omens darkened every sacrifice;
Blood flowed from wells, and through the lofty towns
Wolves' howling voices echoed all night long.
No other time has seen more flashes fall
From cloudless sky, more deadly comets blaze.
So once again the Roman battle lines
Clashed in civil war at Philippi;
The gods saw fit to fatten up once more
The plains of Macedonia with our blood.
And to those places there will come a day
When a farmer drives his curved plough through the
    earth
And strikes on Roman javelins worn with rust,
Or clinks an empty helmet with his spade,
And wonders at the massive bones laid bare.
O my country's gods, my homeland's heroes,
And Romulus, and Vesta, who protect

The Tuscan Tiber, Roman Palatine:
May our young Octavian Caesar right this world
That our disastrous age has overturned!
We have atoned in full for perjured Troy,
And long enough has heaven's court complained
That Caesar celebrates his triumphs here
On earth, where right and wrong have been reversed.
So many wars, so many shapes of crime!
The plough dishonored, fields left lying waste
Now that their men are drafted; curving scythes
Are pounded into shape for ruthless swords.
War in Germany, and in the East:
Neighboring towns dissolve their legal bonds,
And march across each other's boundaries.
Unholy Mars bends all to his mad will:
The world is like a chariot run wild
That rounds the course unchecked and, gaining speed,
Sweeps the helpless driver on to his doom.

BOOK TWO

Our theme so far has dealt with husbandry
And heaven's stars. Now, Bacchus, I shall sing
Of you and of the woodlands, of the shrubs,
Of the slowly growing olive's progeny.
Approach, Lenaean Father: here all things
Are brimming with your gifts, for you the farmlands
Flourish, large with Autumn's trailing vine,
The vintage foams in swelling vats. Approach,
Lenaean Father, lay your shoes aside,
With me plunge naked legs in new-pressed wine.

    Nature, first of all, is versatile
In growing trees, for some rise by themselves
Without man's help, to occupy the fields
And border curving streams, like pliant osier,
Limber broom, the poplar, willow beds
Pale grey with silver leaves; and some spring up
From fallen seed: tall chestnuts, common oaks
Whose leafy shade best shelters sacred groves,
And the durmast-oaks that Greeks believe prophetic.
With others, heavy underbrush grows up

From parent roots, like cherry trees and elms;
The small Parnassian laurel takes her place
Beneath her mother's massive shade. These methods
Nature first devised, and by them grows
Each kind of forest, shrub and sacred wood.

    Other means experience has found.
One man has a way of tearing slips
From their mothers' tender body, setting them
In furrows, while another buries stems
In ground as crosscut poles or pointed stakes.
And some trees wait for layers to be bent
And, arching, draw their life from native soil.
Still others need no root, and pruners snip
The upper sprays, consign them to the ground.
Incredibly, when olive trunks are split
A root will push its way from the dried-out stem.
We notice too that one tree branches off
To fasten on another, unrebuked:
The transformed pear producing grafted apples,
Stony cornels reddening on the plum.

    Come then, farmers, learn to grow each type
As suits it best, domesticate wild fruits
By raising them: let not your land lie idle.
What joy it is to sow all Thrace with vines
And clothe in olive the slope of vast Taburnus!

O worthy friend, to whom my reputation
Is most due, Maecenas, bear with me
In the work at hand; unfurl the flying sails
To the spreading sea. I choose not to enfold
All things within my verse, not though I had
A hundred tongues and mouths, a voice of iron.
Now come with me and cruise along the shore;
Land is in reach: I'll not detain you here
With fancied themes, digressions, overtures.

 Some trees of their own accord ascend
The shores of light, and grow up hail and strong,
Although unfruitful; nature's vital force
Pervades the soil. And even they will shed
Their jungle spirits if a man transplants
Them into ready trenches, or makes grafts,
And under constant care they swiftly learn
To follow any methods you devise.
A barren slip that comes from roots deep down
In a stem would do this too if amply spaced
In open field, but now the mother's boughs
And leafy depths obscure it, and deprive
The growing tree of fruit, consume its yield.
The tree that rises up from random seed
Grows slowly, and will one day furnish shade
To children of a later age: its fruits

Degenerate, forget their former taste,
The vine bears sorry clusters, loot for birds.
So, labor makes demands in ceaseless flow
That trees must be controlled at heavy cost
And forced in grooves. But olives best respond
To trunks, and vines to layers, Venus' myrtle
To solid stems. From slips the hardwood hazel
Comes to life, the mighty ash, shade-poplars
(Hercules' crown), Dodonian oaks. High palms
Grow likewise, and the fir that soon will see
The perils of the deep. But rough arbutus
Grafts with walnut shoots, and sterile planes
Do well with sturdy apples, beech looks white
With chestnut blossoms, ash goes pale with pears,
And pigs crunch acorns underneath the elms.
There are several ways to graft or set in buds
For where the buds protrude from core of bark
And burst the tender sheath, a narrow groove
Is made just at the knot; here men insert
A bud from a different tree which they instruct
To grow into the gummy bark; or else
A cut is made in smoothly surfaced trunks
And a path is wedged deep into solid bole
Where the fertile shoots are thrust; and soon enough
A mighty tree spreads skyward joyous boughs,

Admires its novel leaves and alien fruits.
    Varieties of valiant elm exist,
Of willow, lotus, or Idaean cypress;
In no one way are fertile olives born
But oval-shaped like orchids, straight like rods,
Or as bitter-berried "pausian." Orchard fruits
Are varied in Alcinous' retreat.
Cuttings differ with the Tuscan pears
And Syrian, and volema's handful weight.
On our trees quite a different vintage dangles
From that which Lesbos plucks off the boughs of
    Methymna.
There are Thasian vines, and Mareotic Whites;
The latter flourish best in fertile soils,
The former suit light land; for raisin wine
Psithian works out well, and sly Lagcan
That soon will trip your feet and tie your tongue;
Some wines are Purples, other Early Ripeners;
How shall I sing your praise, O Rhaetian draft?
And still, you cannot match Falernian vaults;
We have as well the Aminean vines
On our western shores, a pure and solid wine
Before whom Tmolian, even Royal Chian
Rise in deference; Argitis Minor,
With which none can compete in quantity

And lasting through the years. I should include
You, Rhodian, most welcome by the gods
And by men at their banquet's second course,
And you, Bumastus, large-breasted, juicy, round.
But, number will not tell the many kinds
Or all their names; nor does the total count;
Whoever wants to know this should inquire
To learn how many particles of sand
The West Wind swirls in Libya's desert plain,
Or how many waves the Ionian Sea hurls shoreward
When the savage East Wind falls on merchant ships.
No single land maintains all kinds of tree:
Willows love streams, but alders grow in swamps;
The barren ash clings to the rocky hills;
Myrtles love the shore, vines open slopes;
Yews like a cold exposure to the North.
Observe the edges of the civil world:
Eastern Arabs, painted Ukraine tribes;
By trees the nations may be told apart.
India grows her jet black ebony
And Arabia Felix boughs of frankincense.
Shall I tell of fragrant, gum-soaked balsams,
Of evergreen acacia? The soft white cotton
In Ethiopian groves? Or how the Chinese
Comb their silk from leaves, or the tangled groves

Of India's seacoast, earth's remotest fold
Whose lofty trees no arrow can surmount
(Although the race is famed for archery)?
Media's bitter herbs, the lingering tang
Of lemon, that no antidote surpasses
When fierce stepmothers brew their deadly drugs—
Commingling herbs and non-innocuous charms—
The Median liquids draw the poison off
And drive the blackened venom from the limbs:
Their tree itself is large, much like the laurel
But for its fragrance, in the blowing wind
The leaves and blossoms hang on hard; the Mede
Employs it to cure asthma in the old,
Distils it as a draft to sweeten breath.

But not the groves of Media, wealthy land,
Nor lovely Ganges, nor the golden streams
Of Lydia match Italy in praise;
Not India, Afghanistan, nor isles
Of Araby with incense-bearing sands.
No fiery bulls ploughed Italy's black soil
To sow a crop of giant dragon's teeth,
No human warriors sprang full-armed from her fields:
But teeming fruit and wine of the Campagna
Filled our Italian fields; fat herds and olives
Found their place in Italy's rich land.

Hence, the charger prancing in the plain;
Hence, white sheep and sacrificial bull,
So often plunged in Umbria's sacred streams,
Precede our Roman triumphs to the temples.
Here Spring persists, and Summer makes her way
Through foreign months: the flocks bear twice a year,
And twice the useful tree yields up her apples;
No raving tigers, savage lion cubs:
No poison wolfsbane fools the poor herb-gatherers.
No scaly reptile hustles huge coils across
The ground—or stops and winds his train in spirals.
See our noble cities, labor's crown,
Built breathlessly upon steep mountainsides,
Deep rivers flowing under ancient walls!
Shall I name the seas on either side?
Our inland lakes—you, Larian Como, the greatest,
And you, oh Garda, whose sea-waves plunge and roar?
Recall the Julian Port at Lake Lucrine
Where the channeled Tyrrhene flows into Avernus,
And the jetties thrust against the indignant sea
With a hissing surge, where Julian water sings
Its distant tones of tidal solitude?
Our land is veined with silver, copper, gold.
Italian soil has bred a race of heroes,
Marsians, Sabines, toughened generations

From the Western Coast, and tribes of Volscians
Handy with the spear. Great family names,
Camillus, Decius, Marius, Scipio,
And, chief of all, Octavianus Caesar,
Who triumphs now on Asia's farthest shore,
And defends the hills of Rome from the timid foe.
All hail, Saturnian Land, our honored Mother!
For thee I broach these themes of ancient art
And dare disclose the sacred springs of verse,
Singing Hesiod's song through Roman towns.
    Now for the innate qualities of soils:
The color, strength, productive powers of each.
Ground that is hard to deal with, awkward hills,
Thin fields of marl, stone-cluttered undergrowths,
Welcome a grove of Pallas' long-lived olives.
Wild olives, cropping out on every side,
And fields strewn thick with berries, mark the place.
But moist and lush terrain, and fertile flatlands
Thick with grass (the sort we see below
In mountain vales where brooks slip down the rocks
And wash in fertile mud), and southern heights
That favor ferns, the bane of curving ploughs,
Will yield you hardy vineyards full of wine:
This soil is good for grapes, and for the juice
We offer to the gods in cups of gold,

As the sleek Etruscan plays his ivory pipe
Beside the altars where we sacrifice
With steaming entrails loaded high on plates.
But if you are more intent on herds and yearlings,
On breeding sheep, on goats that ruin crops,
Seek out the distant plains of rich Tarentum
And meadows like those lost to Mantua
That nourish snow-white swans on river-grass;
Your flocks need running springs and pasturage,
And what the herds crop off on summer days
The cool dew will restore in slender nights.
The land that's black and rich beneath the plough
The crumbling soil we reproduce in ploughing,
Is best for grain (from here you'll often see
Oxen lumbering home with wagons full);
Or land where an irate ploughman wrecks the woods
And levels copses idle many years,
Tears from their roots the ancient homes of birds:
They leave their nests behind and soar aloft;
But the raw earth gleams beneath the driving plough.
Famished gravel land in hilly districts
Hardly offers stunted spurge for bees,
Or rosemary; and scaling tufa, chalk beds
Tunnelled through and through by blackskinned snakes,
Are peerless for providing winding lairs,

Outclassing other grounds, as they supply
The serpents with a dainty choice of food.
The soil that breathes forth wisps of floating fog,
That drinks in dampness, drains it off at will,
And wears a grassy robe of evergreen
Yet never scores your tools with flakes of rust,
This soil will weave your elms with joyous vines
And yield an olive crop, and it will prove
When cultivated, gracious to the herd,
Submissive to the ploughshare's curving blade.
Such arable rich Capua enjoys
And the coast that borders on Vesuvius' ridge
Where the Garigliano drifts past lone Acerrae.

   Now I shall teach you to distinguish soils.
If you want looser earth, or more close-packed,
(The latter favors grain, the former wine)
Inspect the place beforehand, dig a hole
Quite deep in solid ground, and then replace
The earth and tamp the crust down with your feet.
If dirt is lacking, then your soil is loose,
Most fit for fertile vines and pasturage;
If the earth will not go back, and overflows
The trench, it's close-packed; so anticipate
A sticking clod and lumpy ridge, and cut in
Furrows with a brace of powerful bulls.

But salty land, and the kind we know as "sour"
(Hard on grain, hard for the plough to tame)
Which ruins vines, makes fruit degenerate,
Submits to proof this way: from smoky rafters
Take some sieves and close-weaved wicker baskets;
Pack the perverse earth in and add spring water
And tread the contents down; of course, the liquid
All escapes, the large drops trickling through;
And when the testers taste the bitter drops,
Their twisting lips make plain the telltale truth.
We learn what soil is rich in the following way:
When tossed from hand to hand, it never crumbles,
Grows sticky, clings like pitch to the handler's fingers
Over-lush wet soil grows grass too tall.
Ah, may my land be never found too rich
And display its strength too early in the blade!
Heavy soils, and light, betray themselves
In silence, by their weight. Your eye is quick
To recognize the black and other colors.
But it's hard to ferret out the fiendish cold:
Occasionally, pitch-pines and noxious yews
Or dark-hued ivy creepers, show it up.

   With this advice in mind, think well ahead,
And bake your land in sunlight, cleave broad hills
With ditches, and expose the upturned clods

To North winds, ere you plant the joyful stocks
Of vine. For fields, a crumbling soil is best;
Winds and icy frosts see after this,
And a sturdy delver, turning up the land.
But men who never let a chance slip by
Choose a site beforehand for the seedlings
To begin their training, like the later site
Of transplantation, that the sudden shift
Of mother may not strike the plant as strange.
They score the heaven's quarters on the bark,
Replacing as it stood the part that faced
The fervid South, the back turned towards the North:
For habit dominates the early stage.
Inquire first whether hills or flats improve
Your vines. And if you mark off plots
Of fertile plain, sow thick: for Bacchus then
Bestirs himself as much for a heavy yield.
Whether you choose the rising ground of knolls,
Or supine hills, deploy the ranks at ease;
And as the trees are set in, let each row
Square nicely to the line and come up true;
As a legion massed for war deploys its ranks,
And halts its columns on an open field
And dresses up the lines: the whole space waves
And weapons flash, but combat still holds off

While dubious Mars roves through opposing ranks.
Create an equal space between the rows:
Not that the vista feed your empty mind,
But since no other way will land give strength
To all, and boughs have open space to grow.

Perhaps you'd like to know how deep to trench.
I'd dare entrust the vines to shallow clefts,
But tree stems must drive deep into the earth,
And most of all the oak, whose shaft soars up
To heaven's vault as high as at the root
She gropes toward Tartarus. No storms, nor blows,
Nor cloudbursts, shake her loose: she dwells steadfast,
Survives your children's children as she spans
The ages human lives endure, outstretching
Right and left her noble boughs and arms,
From her central self supports a massive shade.

Your vine slopes must avoid the setting sun,
You should not set in hazels by the vines,
Nor (since they love the earth so ardently)
Cut high switches, tear off upper twigs,
Nor bruise the slips with blunt iron instruments,
Nor plant wild olive stems among the vines.
For often careless shepherds drop a spark
That, stealthily at first, hides in the wood
Beneath the oily bark, and then escapes

To catch the upper leaves and crackle skyward;
And takes its path to triumph over boughs
And treetop, folding all the grove in flames,
And, thick with pitch-black smoke, shoots up a cloud
Of streaming darkness, worst of all when a storm
Falls straight down on the forest, and the wind
Corrals and spreads the flames. When this occurs,
The vines have no strength left them at the root,
Cut back, cannot recover, nor grow green
From deep in earth as formerly; the barren,
Bitter-leaved wild-olive takes their place.

    Let no adviser, prudent as may be,
Persuade you to disturb the stiffened earth
When North winds blow. Then Winter closes off
The ice-bound countryside, will not permit
The broadcast seed to pierce the hardened ground.
The best seed-time for vines is blushing Spring,
When first appears the white bird long snakes loathe;
Or first Fall frosts, before the hot Sun's team
Has yet reached Winter, but summertime has come
And gone. Spring fills the groves with leaves,
Is good to forests; earth expands in the Spring,
And sends out calls for life-inspiring seed.
Then Heaven, the father almighty, comes down to
    earth

In pregnant rains to embrace his joyous bride,
Infusing her massive frame with vital strength.
Then pathless thickets ring with songs of birds,
And herds comply with Venus' set demands;
The kindly field gives birth, and furrowed lands
Release their folds to the West Wind's ruffling breeze;
Soft moisture floods all things, the green blades dare
To face the newborn suns, the budding vines
Have no fear of the South Wind's springing up,
Nor of rain the North Wind lashes through the sky.
But put forth buds, unfolding all their leaves.
Days like these shone on our growing world
In its beginnings, then to such a course
They held, in my belief; for that was Spring,
The great world lived in Spring perpetual,
And East winds held in check their wintry blasts,
When the first beasts drank in light, and a race of men
Earth-born, reared its hardy head from the fields:
When beasts were loose in the woods and stars in the
    sky.
Nor could such fragile things have borne this toil
Unless a long repose divided cold
From heat, and heaven's grace restored the earth.
   As for the rest, whatever slips you set
In fields, be sure to sprinkle well with dung

And cover well with earth or bury in
With porous stone, rough-surfaced shells: for water
Filters in between, and the slender air
Will breathe below, and the plants will lift their hearts.
Some have been known to lay on top a weight
Of heavy stones and pots which forms a shield
Against the pelting rains and sultry star
That splits the gaping furrows wide with thirst.
      With all the plants in place, it still remains
To shift the earth about their roots quite often,
To swing your heavy hoe, and work the earth
Beneath the ploughshare's weight, and drive your bulls
Straining in between the vineyard's rows;
Then, to shape smooth canes and stripped-down poles,
And stakes of ash and sturdy, two-pronged forks,
That, leaning on their strength the vines may learn
To scorn the winds, climb highest flights of elms.
      But while the first youth sprouts upon the leaves
Bear with their weakness; while the vine shoot plunges
Toward the sky in joy, propelled through space
With reins relaxed, it must not be assailed
By the knife's keen edge; nip off the leaves by hand,
And with curving fingers pick them here and there.
But when they've grown and clasp with sturdy stem
The elms, then clip their hair and shear their arms

(Before this time they fear the steel), assert
Your harsh controls and check the flowing boughs.
    Weave hedges too, and keep out all the herds,
When the leaf is tender, ignorant of work.
For besides unfeeling winters, tyrant suns,
Wild buffaloes and pestering wild roe
Make sport with leaves, and sheep and greedy heifers
Eat them up. And rigid, frostbound cold
Or heavy heat that dwells on burning crags
Do less harm than those flocks, whose raking teeth
Are poison, leaving scars along the roots.
For just this guilt, a goat is sacrificed
To Bacchus at each shrine, and tragedies
Of old came on the stage, and Theseus' sons
Gave prizes out for local wit in towns
And crossroads, and they danced in mellow fields
On well-oiled goatskins, tipsy; and Ausonians,
A people sent from Troy to settle here,
Sport their disheveled verses, crude guffaws,
And don their grisly masks of hollow cork
And sing to you, O Bacchus, happy songs,
And hang your swaying mask on lofty pines,
That as the god inclines his noble head
In each direction, ripening vineyards grow,
Hollow vales and deepened glades fill out.

We shall, then, sing, in native songs, our debt
Of praise to Bacchus, bring on cakes and plates
And lead in by the horns a sacred goat
To stand beside the altar, and proceed
To roast his fertile flesh on hazel spits.
    Another task in looking after vines
Is never finished: several times a year
Our hoes slice into soil, and then reversed,
Their upper edges smash the clods apart
Continually, and we clear the groves of leaves.
The farmers' work returns to them full circle—
Their year revolves, retracing its own steps.
And now, the vineyard sheds its final leaves,
When freezing North winds shake the glory loose
From the woods. And even then the country man,
Keen at heart, extends his care to meet
The coming year, pursues the vine he has left,
And pares it back with Saturn's curving knife,
And prunes it into shape. So, be the first
To spade the ground, the first to carry off
And burn the prunings, first to get your poles
In under cover; be the last to pick.
Twice, the shade will thicken on your vines,
Twice, the weeds will clutter up your vineyards
Dense and brambly; both these tasks are hard:

Admire a large estate but work a small one.
In the forest, too, rough shoots of broom are cut
And reeds on river banks; neglected willows
Call for care. But now the vines are bound,
The pruning knife laid down: the last vine-dresser
Sings a song of finished rows: but still,
The earth must be harassed, the dust disturbed,
Jove's rains on ripened grapes must cause alarm.
    Olives, on the other hand, are easy:
They need no crooked knife, no grasping rakes,
Once they cling to fields and brave the air,
The earth herself, laid bare by the hoe's curved fang,
Supplies sufficient moisture for the plants,
And, bared by ploughing, brings on heavy fruit.
So raise the plump round olive, dear to Peace.
    Fruit trees, too, when first they feel secure
Within their stems and know their strength, shoot up
And struggle skyward of their own accord
And need no help from us. The wildwood, too,
Is laden down with fruit, and the jumbled groves
Where birds nest blush with berries. Cattle feed
On clover, lofty pine woods furnish logs,
The fires of night are fed and pour forth light:
Do men delay to sow and lavish pains?
But why pursue this talk of the larger trees?

Our lowly broom, our willow, furnish herds
With leaves or shepherds with a shade, or crops
With fences, honey with its food. And what a joy
It is to see Cytorus in the East
With rippling boxwood, Locri in our South
With pitch-pine groves, and what a joy it is
To look on fields that owe no obligation
To the hoe, none to the hand of man!
Even sterile woods on Caucasian heights
That angry East winds ever toss and tear
Give one thing or another for our use:
They furnish pines for building ships, and cypress
For our homes, and cedarwood. From these
The farmers fashion rounded spokes for wheels,
Or solid drums for wagons, and from these
They lay broad keels for ships. The willow's wealth
Lies in her reeds, the elm's lies in her leaves,
But myrtles, and the cherry, good for war,
Make strong spear shafts, and yew trees may be bent
To shape Ituraean bows. Smooth linden trees
And boxwood, too, turned on the lathe, take shape.
Light alders bob along the spinning Po,
And bees can house their swarms in hollow bark
Or in the belly of a rotting oak.
What gifts to equal these has Bacchus borne?

Bacchus even gives us cause for blame:
He brought the raging Centaurs to their doom,
Rhoetus, Pholus, violent Hylaeus
Who menaced Lapiths with a mighty bowl.
 Oh that farmers understood their blessings!
Their boundless joys! A land far off from war
Pours forth her fruit abundantly for them.
Although no stately home with handsome portals
Disgorges on its step a wave of callers
Every morning, gaping at his doors
Inlaid with tortoise shell, astonished by
His gold-trimmed clothes and his Corinthian bronzes,
Although his white wool is not stained with dye,
His oil not spoiled with perfumes from the East,
His rest is sound, his life devoid of guile.
His gains are manifold, his holdings broad:
Caves and living lakes, refreshing vales,
The cattle lowing, slumber in the shade.
Familiar with the haunts of animals,
The farmer lives in peace, his children all
Learn how to work, respect frugality,
Venerate their fathers and the gods:
Surely, Justice, as she left the earth,
In parting left her final traces here.
 And as for me, may first the sweet-toned Muses,

Whose symbols I raise up, inspired by love,
Find me worthy, spread before my eyes
The planets and the stars, the sun's eclipses,
The moon's revolving labors, the earthquake's source;
Reveal the hidden motions of the sea,
That force the waters up and sink them down.
Show why the winter suns race toward the Ocean,
What holds in check the long-delaying nights.
But if I fail to master nature's lore
Because cold-blooded humors slow my mind,
Still, let me relish the country, humbly revere
Streams that glide through glades, the woods, the rivers.
Oh, for Thessalian plains, for your Swirling Stream,
Or Taygetus' slopes that Spartan girls traverse
In Bacchic revel! Oh, to be wafted away
And placed amid the frost-cool vales of Haemus,
Shielded and soothed by the branches' generous shade!
Blessed is he who masters nature's laws,
Tramples on fear and unrelenting fate,
On greedy, roaring Acheron. But happy
Too is he who knows the gods of nature,
Old man Silvanus, Pan, the sister nymphs.
Not for him "the mandate of the people,"
The royal cloak of kings, not dissonance
Creating civil wars, the swift onslaught

From Balkan coalitions; not for him
The Roman State or Empires doomed to die.
He grieves not for the poor nor hates the rich.
The boughs by their own virtue bear him fruit,
He gathers what the willing fields supply;
Has not made contact with our ironclad laws,
Our frantic Forum, our Public Record Office.
Others lash the unknown seas with oars,
Rush at the sword, pay court in royal halls.
One destroys a city and its homes
To drink from jeweled cups and sleep on scarlet;
One hoards his wealth and lies on buried gold.
One gapes dumbfounded at the speaker's stand;
At the theater, still another, open-mouthed,
Reels before crescendos of applause
From the tiers where mob and dignitaries sit.
Others are keen to drench themselves in blood,
Their brothers' blood, and, exiled, change their homes
And winsome hearths, to range abroad for room
To live in, underneath a foreign sun.

   The farmer drives his curved plough through the
      earth:
His year's work lies in this; thus he sustains
His homeland, his diminutive descendants,
His herds of stock, his much-deserving bullocks.

Without repose, the overflowing seasons
Bring in apples, and increase the flock;
Wheat sheaves load the furrows, burst the barns.
Then Winter comes, the mills are pressing olives,
The pigs come home rejoicing, stuffed with acorns,
Strawberries crop out in forest groves.
Autumn places varied fruits before us,
As the mellow vineyard basks in hillside heat.
Meanwhile, sweet children hang on the farmer's kisses,
His decent home preserves its purity;
Cows' udders bulge with milk, and the rotund kids
Lock horns in combat waged on luxuriant lawns.
The master takes a holiday, stretched out
On the grass among his friends around a fire:
They weave a wreath for the drinking-bowl, while he
Summons you, Lenaeus, with libation,
Then places on the elm, for the shepherds' aim,
A target for flashing javelins; they strip bare
Their hardened bodies for a rural wrestling match.
Such a life the Sabines once embraced,
And Romulus and Remus; in this way
Etruria grew strong; thus Rome was formed,
Surpassing in beauty, when she first enclosed
All seven of her hills with a single wall.
Saturn led this golden life on earth

Before Jove ruled in Crete, and long before
A guilty race made meals of slaughtered bullocks:
When men had never heard the bugles blow
Nor sword blades clatter on stubborn anvil-irons.

But now we have traversed a widespread plain:
It is time to free our horses' steaming necks.

BOOK THREE

Now we shall sing the shepherds' rural gods,
Recall Apollo's role in guarding herds,
And sing the woods and rivulets of Pan.
All other themes are stale, diverting tunes
To while the time away. We know these tales
By heart: severe Eurystheus, grim Busiris,
Handsome Hylas, Delos-isled Latona,
Ivory-shouldered, master-horseman Pelops,
Who won his bride by murdering her father.
I must find a way to soar aloft
And raise my verse above this common soil,
To fly victorious on the lips of men.
If life allow, my epic verse will show
The Muses have left Helicon for Rome;
I shall be the first to bring to you,
O Mantua, the palms of victory;
And, beside the noble Mincio's sinuous stream
That takes its wandering course past reed-lined banks,
Build a marble shrine on the verdant plain.
Within my temple Caesar will hold sway.

And I, set off by purple robes as victor,
Will lead, to honor him, processional ranks
Of a hundred four-horse chariots past the shore.
For me all Greece will leave behind Alpheus,
And Nemean groves, to try their fortunes here
In races, in the rawhide boxing bouts.
I myself, adorned with olive wreath,
Will proffer gifts. Now, even now, I feel
The joy of leading solemn throngs to the shrines
Or of seeing bullocks slain in sacrifice;
Or, seated at the drama's shifting scenes,
Of observing how the forms of captive Britons,
Inwoven, seem to raise the purple curtains.
On the temple doors, from gold and solid ivory
I will carve the Ganges, overpowered by Rome;
Elsewhere the swelling Nile, full flood with war,
And columns formed from prows of captured ships.
The sculpture I design will show the vanquished
Asian and Armenian mountain heights,
Retreating Parthians, shooting arrows back,
The double trophies seized from far-flung foes
Of both worlds: Roman wins in East and West.
Marble statues, supple and alive,
Will show our Trojan forebears, sprung from Jove:
Father Tros, Apollo founding Troy,

Ill-favored Envy, cowed by Hell's harsh stream,
The Furies, and Ixion's twisting snakes,
And Sisyphus' insuperable stone.
Meanwhile, let us trace the dryads' steps
Through woods and virgin forests, following
Your firm requests, Maecenas: without you,
My mind could not conceive a lofty theme.
Now up and off! Cithaeron loudly calls,
And Spartan hounds, horsetaming Epidaurus;
And the forest, brought alive with hunting sounds,
Voices assent, re-echoing back the cry.
Later, I shall don the epic robes,
To sing of Caesar's fiery wars, extend
His name as far in future years as now
It traces back to Troy its origins.

    Whoever raises horses to compete
In games or breeds stout bullocks for the plough
Should choose the mothers' bodies carefully.
The best-formed cow looks fierce, her head is coarse,
Her neck is large, her dewlaps hang down loose
From throat to shank; flanks rangy as you wish,
And largeness through the limbs, including feet,
Are preferable, and look for shaggy ears
Below the crooked horns. Nor do I mind
If she shows spots of white, resents the yoke,

And flourishes her horns, and if her face
Looks like a bull's, and if she is very tall,
With a tail that sweeps the tracks she leaves behind.

    Commencing with the fifth, the years for mating
End before the tenth, and other years
She is fit for neither breeding nor the plough.
So, while the herd rejoices in its youth,
Release the males and breed the cattle early,
Supply one generation from another.
For mortal kind, the best day passes first:
Disease and sad old age come on, and work;
The ruthless grasp of death ensnares us all!
There will always be some stock you would exchange:
Replace them promptly, sorting out the young
Within the herd, beforehand, year by year,
That later on you may not feel the loss.

    In principle, the same applies to horses.
But here you must take special pains at first
Toward the foals whom you propose as sires.
The foal of noble strain stands out at once
As, prancing through the fields, he raises high
His slender legs and plants them down again;
He takes the lead and fords a threatening stream,
Trusts an unknown bridge, will never shy
At empty sounds. His markings are: high neck,

A tapering head, short belly, rounded back;
The muscles of his proud chest ripple well
(Roans and greys are best, and whites and duns
The worst in color). Then, if armor rattles
From afar, he will not stay in place,
Pricks up his ears and quivers in his limbs,
Rolls out a fiery breath beneath his nose.
His mane lies thick, tossed over on the right;
The ridge is double in between his loins,
And earth rings hollow with the heavy beat
From his hoof of solid horn. Such steeds as these
Were Cyllarus, with Pollux for his master,
The horses our Greek poets celebrate,
The brace of Mars, and great Achilles' pair.
In such a form swift Saturn tossed the mane
Across his neck when Rhea found him, fled
Up Pelion, and his shrill neighs filled the heights.
   Shut in an ailing creature, one weighed down
With illness, or retarded by the years,
Show no compassion for disgraceful age.
The old horse but prolongs the agony
Of love, from his frigidity; in war,
His rage is wild but weak as stubble fire.
First, note his age and spirit, mark them well;
And then his other merits, pedigree,

Remorse when outclassed, pride in victory.
Have you not seen them fighting for the lead,
Their chariots plunging when the barrier drops,
The drivers' surging hopes, the pounding fear
That drains exulting hearts? They close in,
Ply the lash, crouch over loosened reins,
The glowing axle spins, the drivers' bodies
Seem now to scrape the ground, and now to soar
Through empty air, wheels rising in the wind;
No hanging back, no rest: a golden cloud
Of sand swirls in their wake, the flecks of foam,
The breath of the pursuers, soak them through:
So great is their love for praise, their will to win.
Athens' ancient king first dared to yoke
Four horses to a chariot; standing up,
He drove victorious toward the goal. The Lapiths
Fitted bridles, trained the cavalry,
Harnessed mounts and taught them how to wheel,
Instructed armored knights to take the jumps
And step out proudly, rounded and firm in pace.
To breed up either type is just as hard:
The master looks for spirit, speed and youth
In equal measure, not regarding times
The old horse put his enemy to flight,
Nor that he claim Epirus or Mycenae

As his birthplace, and an ancestry from Neptune.
  With all these things in mind, as time draws near,
They lavish pains to round out fat and sleek
The horse they choose to lead and sire the herd;
They mow fresh hay and bring him grain and water,
That he perform his pleasant task with power,
That weak sons may not show an ill-fed father.
They underfeed the mares intentionally,
And when familiar yearnings turn their minds
To mating, they are kept off leaves and water.
They run them ragged, tire them in the heat,
While the threshing floor groans under heavy flails,
And the empty chaff is tossed to rising winds.
This prevents the warm, life-giving field
From being dulled to use by surplus ease
And choked with sluggish furrows, but provides
That, thirsty, it shall grasp Love, hide it deep.
  But now the mothers' needs supplant the fathers'.
When, weighted with the months, they roam abroad,
They must not be allowed to bear the weight
Of yokes and wagons, nor to leap the road,
Nor race through pastures, swim the rushing streams.
They feed in quiet clearings, by the banks
Of brimming rivers, mossy, lush with grass,
And grottoes where projecting rocks give shade.

Amid Lucania's evergreen oak forests
Gadflies swarm, in Latin called "Asilus,"
In Greek, the *oistros*, buzzing harsh and sharp,
That rout the herds in panic through the woods;
The bellowings rage across the blasted air
Through woodlands, to the dried-out Tangro's shore.
Once Juno wrought her terrifying wrath
On Io, plotting ruin by this pest.
So shield your pregnant flock, and since the fly
Is worst at noon, turn out the herds at dawn
Or when the guiding stars lead nightfall on.

    With birth, all interest turns upon the young;
They sear the brand and parentage on those
Reserved for breeding, set apart as sacred
To altars, or reserved to cut the earth
And transform well-ridged plains with broken clods.
The rest are put to browse the emerald grass:
Now, those you will develop, train, and use
For husbandry, launch early on the path
Of discipline, while youthful minds are plastic,
While the age is flexible. And first, entwine
Loose leading-strings of osier round their necks;
And when free necks grow used to servitude,
Harness pairs with these same plaited ropes,
Insist that they keep step; and have them draw

The empty carts cross-country, tracing lightly
On the crust. Then later, beechwood axles
Should strain and creak beneath their heavy load,
And the bronze shaft drag the harnessed wheels along.
Meanwhile, you will pick not only grass
For the untamed calves, fen-sedge and willow leaves,
But planted grain; nor should the mother cows
Fill pails with snowy milk, as custom bids,
But spend the whole bag on their darling sons.

   But if you relish wars and fighting groups,
Or like to glide past Pisa's stream, Alpheus,
Or race your chariots through the sacred grove:
The horse's task is, first, to know the sight
Of arms and of gallant men, to stand the blast
Of trumpets, bear the noise of grating wheels.
To hear the harness jingling in his stall;
Then more and more to joy in his master's praise,
To love the sound of patting on his neck.
Let him attempt this when he is weaned, then trust
His mouth to soft rope halters, while he is weak
And trembling, unfamiliar as yet with life.
But when, three summers passed, the fourth is nigh,
Let him start to pace the ring with measured steps,
To bend his legs in alternating curves,
Take on the air of work; then let him race

Against the wind, fly over open fields
As if the reins were off, and scarcely leave
His hoofmarks on the surface of the sand,
Like a gathered wind that swoops down from the
  North,
Scattering Russia's arid clouds and squalls:
The floating plains and wheatfields tremble lightly
From the gusts, and treetops sigh aloud,
And curling breakers drive in toward the shore;
Just so, he sweeps the fields and plains in flight.
This horse will sweat to reach the finish line
At Elis, as he pounds across the stretch,
His mouth blood-flecked and foaming, or will draw
With supple neck a chariot of war.
Broken in, increase their mighty frames
With coarsened mash; their noble spirits soar
Before they are mastered: caught, they will not obey
The cruel bit, endure the pliant lash.
    Whichever species you prefer to use,
The horse or ox, no effort more conserves
Their strength than freedom from the goads of lust.
So, bulls are sent far off to browse alone
Behind the hill, across a widened stream,
Or kept in their stalls at well-stocked feeding troughs.
For gradually the female wastes his strength,

Inflames him by her sight, with her allurement
Dims his memory of groves and grasses,
And often forces two impassioned lovers
To decide the issue for themselves with horns.
   A lovely heifer grazed in Southern Sila:
Two rival champions clashed with shocking force,
Wounds followed, thick and fast, the gore flowed free,
As locked horns twisted, strained, and creaked and
     groaned;
The woods and outspread heavens rocked with sound.
The warriors now refuse to herd together,
The loser slinks off into isolation
By some unknown shore, enumerates his woes,
His loss of face, the haughty victor's blows,
The passion unavenged: and looking back,
Deserts his father's kingdom: thereupon,
He nurses back his strength, and perseveres
On rocky beds, on nourishment of brambles
And sharp reed grass, and tests himself, and learns
To whet his horns in rage against tree trunks,
Feints lunging at the air, and scores the sand
In mock encounters. Then, with gathered force
And rebuilt strength, he brings the guidon up
And thunders down on his forgetful foe:
As a wave begins to whiten in mid-sea,

Gathers up its folds from deep below,
And, curling landward, crashes on the rocks,
Like a falling mountain mass; the whirling depths
Tear loose and hurl aloft the muddy sand.

    Thus, every living creature, man and beast,
The ocean's tribes, the herds, the colorful birds,
Rush toward the furious flames: love levels all.
More savage than at any other time,
The lioness leaves her cubs to rove abroad,
And awkward bears wreak havoc through the woods.
The boar is fierce, the tiger at his worst:
A bad time to be straying all alone
In Africa! You have noticed horses trembling
When their nostrils catch the all-familiar scent?
No reins or savage whips can hold them in,
No crags or yawning cliffs can block their path,
No mountain-lifting river's flood-tide wave.
The Sabine boar in frenzy whets his tusks,
Paws at the earth and rubs his flanks on trees,
Toughening up his shoulders, back and front.
What of cruel love's consuming fire
That fans the flames deep in Leander's heart?
He swims the storm-tossed straits in blackest night
And above him thunder splits the ports of sky

While the waters crash and plunge on the cliff-lined
   shore.
His heartsick parents cannot call him back,
Nor can his maiden, spared for her cruel end.
What of Bacchus' leopards, ferocious breeds
Of wolves and dogs? The peaceful deer at war?
   The rage of mares surpasses all the rest,
And Venus surely gave them this intent
Once long ago, when Glaucus' thoroughbreds
Went mad and crunched their driver's bones to bits.
Love leads them on across the roaring waves
Of Ascanius, across Mount Ida's range,
Overcoming mountains, swimming streams.
When once the hidden flame has pierced their marrow
(In Spring, since then the warmth flows back to bones),
The mares on lofty crags turn facing West
To catch the breeze, and often, by the wind,
Miraculously conceive without their mates;
Then dash off through the ridges, rocks, and vales,
Not where the Sun or you, East Wind, arise,
But North and West, or where the jet-black South
Is born to grieve the sky with chilling rain.
These mares at mating time secrete a juice
The shepherds rightly call "hippomanes,"
That oozes from the groin, "hippomanes,"

Which grim stepmothers utilize for drugs,
Commingling herbs and non-innocuous charms.
   But time slides past, slides past beyond recall,
While, spellbound, we drift off among details.
Thus far, I have mentioned herds: now for the rest,
I tend the wooly flocks and hairy goats.
Here is work, but fame for you as well,
Believe me, stalwart farmer friends of mine.
I know full well how hard a task it is
To crown with honor such a crabbed theme;
But love transports me to Parnassus' heights:
I yearn to make the steep ascent where none
Has gone before, to make my own smooth path
Down Poetry's Summit to her sacred source.
Now let us hail the shepherds' goddess Pales,
As we assume a broad, majestic tone.
   First I bid you line the sheepfold well
With tender, fresh-mown grass for the sheep to crop
Till summer comes again, and pad the ground
With straw and fern by handfuls, so no ice
Congeal their feet, and damage them with rot.
Next, I bid you satisfy the goats
With leafy shrubs, and pails of pure, fresh water;
Place the pens to catch the winter sun,
Away from wind and February rain

Lowering when Aquarius fades from view.
The more attentive care we give our goats,
The larger the reward (though Eastern wool,
Dyed purple, fetches quite a handsome price);
From a healthy herd of goats come healthy kids
And a good supply of milk: the more we draw
Off foaming, from the udder to the pail,
The more flows richly when we milk again.
Most herdsmen clip the beards and hoary chins
And shear the bristles, useful as tent canvas
And sailcloth for the wretched mariners.
Goats graze along the summits of Arcadia,
Among high-clinging brakes and thorny briars;
They come in of their own accord at night,
And stagger to the stalls with milk bags full.
So take precautions, screen them from the frost
And wintry blasts, and, since they need so little,
Bring them food and branches, leave the lofts
Of hay wide open all the Winter long.
When Summer's West Wind sounds its joyful tones
Lead all your flocks to glades and pasturelands:
Catch the country frost with the morning star,
When day is new, the grass still white, the dew
A sweet delight to herds. At the dry fourth hour,
When plaintive crickets burst the shrubs with song,

I bid you take the flocks to drink from wells
Or pools supplied by weathered oaken troughs;
In midday heat, conduct them to some dale
Where Jove's great oak spreads out his giant branch,
Or somber groves of holms give sacred shade.
Now, once more water them, and feed them
Until, at sundown, evening's cooling breeze
Moderates the air, and a moistening moon
Restores the groves with cool and limpid dew,
When inland copses ring with finches' song
And coasts vibrate with calls of halcyon.

   Now, shall my verse pursue the Libyan nomads,
Their pastures, huts, their scattered settlements?
Their flocks will often, day and night for a month,
Roam and graze the empty tracts and find
No shelter in the vast expanse of land.
This African shepherd takes his world along,
His household, weapons, dog, his bow and arrows,
Much like the Roman soldier fierce in arms
Who marches forth, unfairly burdened down
By all his field equipment, and arrives
Ahead of time, to catch the foe off guard.

   Far otherwise is life among the Russians,
By the Sea of Azov, where the Danube swirls
With yellow silt, and Rhodopé leans North.

These people keep their herds penned up in stalls
For grass is never seen, nor leaves on trees;
The shapeless land lies steeped in drifts of snow,
And piles of ice rise seven meters high.
Winter lasts forever, North winds rage.
The sun can never pierce the shadowy mists:
Not when behind his steeds he mounts the sky,
Not when in Ocean's crimson tide he bathes
His plunging car. And quickly ice films form
On flowing streams; where sailboats used to glide
The wave is host to roomy carts, supports
On its back their ironclad wheels; and brass jars burst
By dozens; clothing just put on grows stiff;
They chop their moisture-bearing wine with axes.
Tarns turn into sheets of solid ice,
Icicles stick to unkempt beards and shine.
Meanwhile, all the air is a mass of snow:
The cattle die, the oxen's heavy frames
Are sheathed in ice; the reindeer herds, jammed close
By the numbing fresh snow mass, can just be seen
Where antler tips protrude; no need of hounds
Or nets or scarlet-feathered leads to cow
The quavering beasts; the natives, sword in hand
Hack down the deer as, blocked by the mountains'
    drifts,

Their chests push vainly forward, kill them off
Still roaring pain, and lug them home with shouts;
While they, secure in ice-caves underground
Kill time, stacking logs beside the hearth
And handing whole elms over to the blaze.
They spend the night at games, as they carouse
On beer and the brew they drink instead of wine.
Clad in shaggy skins and animal furs,
These wild men live beneath the Northern Bear
And take the brunt of heavy Eastern winds.

   If wool concerns you, have no briars, burs,
Or brushwood near; avoid rank feeding-grounds,
Select your flock for soft and snowy fleece.
But if your ram, however dazzling white,
Shows black beneath his palate-moistened tongue,
Reject him, lest he stain the new flock's wool
With darkish spots; pick out another ram
From the crowded field. For, if this is worth belief,
Arcadian Pan, with the lure of a snow-white fleece
Once tricked you, Luna, called on you to come
To his deep-drawn grove, then made you captive
   there,
And you did not disdain the god who called.

   Let him whose love is milk bring in by hand
Sweet clover and lucerne and salt-tinged grass

And lay them in the pens; his goats will drink
Most avidly, and the more swell out their teats;
Their milk will have a subtle salty tang.
Most shepherds keep the new kids from the dams
And fasten iron-spiked muzzles on their mouths.
The milk they draw at dawn and during day,
They cheese at night; but what they draw at dark,
They pour in jars, to carry into town
Where the shepherd makes his way the following morn,
Or lay aside, well salted down, for Winter.
    Don't overlook the task of choosing dogs,
But breed some nimble Spartan pups, some fierce
Molossian hounds. And feed them well on whey.
With guards like these patrolling round your barns
You'll fear no prowling thieves, or raiding wolves,
Or Spanish bandits pouncing on your back.
You will start the shy wild-ass, and course the hare,
And hunt the roe with these dogs; with the pack in cry,
Drive the boar from his marshy lair, through uplands
Shouting, force a huge stag toward the nets.
    You must learn to cleanse the stalls with pungent
        cedar,
To smoke out water snakes, with fumes of gum.
The viper, foul to the touch, likes dirty sheds,
Where he takes refuge, in fear, from the light of day.

The adder (dire for cattle as he is),
Takes shelter there, infects the herd with poison.
My shepherd, lay your hands on a rock or stick,
To strike at the upraised, swollen, hissing neck.
But look! He slithers off, his head tucked in,
Lengthening out, the last slow folds uncoiling!
Calabrian grasslands breed an evil snake,
Whose spiraling breast shows off a scaly back
And tapering belly flecked with massive spots:
As long as spring-fed streams are flowing full
And the land is drenched with vernal Southern rains,
This rascal lives near ponds and river banks
And crams his black maw with fish and loquacious
    frogs;
But when the swamps dry out, and earth lies parched
And gaping in the heat, he darts ashore,
Where, eyes ablaze, he rages through the fields
Wild with thirst, in terror at the heat.
May it never enter my mind to embrace soft sleep
Outdoors at such a time, and lay my length
In a grassy grove when he glides up, all new
And shining from his slough, who leaves at home
His eggs or young and, now superb in the sun,
Shoots from his mouth that flickering, three-forked
    tongue.

But here I would instruct you in the causes
And symptoms of disease. The filthy mange
Attacks your sheep when icy rain and frost
Sink in, or after shearing, when the sweat
Sticks to their hides in clots, and tangled briars
Lacerate their flesh. The masters, therefore,
Plunge the whole flock into flowing rivers:
The ram, with fleece soaked through, floats down the
    stream;
Or bathe the new-sheared bodies with solution
Of bitter olive lees, and mix a salve
Of silver, virgin sulphur, Eastern pitch,
Emollient wax, squills, hellebore, bitumen.
The remedy of steel will cure these sores:
Cut the festering scab away with a knife;
If left alone, the evil flourishes,
While the pious shepherd will not medicate
But keeps hands off, relying on the gods
To rectify the ill. And when the pain
Drives sharply to the bones of bleating lambs,
And parching fever preys upon their limbs—
To stem the raging heat, you lance the wound
And draw the blood from a vein beside the hoof,
As Thracians do, or hardy Russian tribes
Who roam the hills and deserts near the Danube,

Drinking milk well-curdled with mares' blood.
When you see a sheep drift off to the gentle shade
Too often, tug the grasstops idly, lag,
Or stretch out prone mid-pasture, or retire
Alone and last as deepening night draws on,
Check the guilt with steel, before contagion
Winds its way through all the careless herd.
Thicker than gales that rock the twisting sea
Are plagues that seize on herds. Diseases take
The whole summer's flock at once, not singling out
The victims one by one, but the herd entire,
Its future hopes, and its whole original stock.
You know this if you have seen the soaring Alps,
The Austrian castle heights, the Illyrian plains,
Now, after many years, a wasteland still,
The pastures, far and wide, unoccupied.

    Plague struck this region, springing down
From a sickened sky that glowed with Autumn heat,
Killed off the herds and all the roving game,
Infected lakes, contaminated grass.
Opposing symptoms followed in their course
Where dire disease pursued the path of death:
For after fiery thirst pulsed through the veins
And shrivelled up the limbs, a fluid humor
Welled inside the body, sapped the bones,

And undermined them slowly, bit by bit.
Midway in the sacrificial rites,
A victim being crowned with the snow-white wreath
Fell dead before the priest's delaying feet.
Or if the priest succeeded with his slaughter
The entrails of the beast would not catch fire,
The seer could work out no prophecy,
The knife that slit the throat showed little blood,
Whose thin dark trickle hardly stained the sand.
The calves died off in droves amid green grass
Or yielded up sweet life beside full mangers;
The dogs went mad, pigs choked in suffocation.
The wretched horse, once victory's pride and joy,
Lost all desire, forgot to eat and drink,
And pawed the ground; his drooping ears are flecked
With a sweat that comes and goes, as cold as death;
His skin, dried-out and taut, resists the touch.
The symptoms show the early stage of death.
But as the plague gains way among the horses,
Their eyes blaze up, their deep and long-drawn breaths
Catch with occasional moans, and heavy sobbing
Racks their flanks, blood gushes from the nose,
The roughened tongue sticks fast against the throat.
It helped somewhat to pour wine through a horn
And down the horses' throats, and such a step

Seemed the sole remaining hope for cure:
But this treatment only hurried on the end,
For fever mounted furiously, and then,
Approaching death, the horses bared their teeth
To tear apart their flesh and crunch their bones.
(May the gods grant loyal men a better lot,
Reserve such madness for our enemies!)
See the bull go down beneath the plough:
Blood flecks his foaming breath, he heaves a groan.
The ploughman frees the live companion bull
Grieving for his brother's death; the plough
Hangs fixed, midway along the half-turned furrow.
No more will lofty shades entice this bull,
No luscious mead, no stream more pure than amber
Tumbling over stones to reach the plain!
His flanks cave in, a drowsy numbness clouds
Across his eyes, his massive neck declines
Drooping of its own weight toward the ground.
Is this the fruit of labor, this the reason
The strong and patient beast has drawn the plough?
No wine, no overeating took their toll:
His simple diet called for grass and leaves,
He drank from limpid pools and racing streams,
No restless cares disturbed his sweet repose.

   Then, they say, for the sole time in these parts,

White cows could not be found for Juno's rites,
And buffaloes, instead, in ill-matched pairs,
Drew chariots to the lofty treasure-house.
Men hacked the ground with rakes, and dug in the seed
With blistered fingers, hitched themselves to carts
And, straining forward, dragged the creaking loads.
Wolves ceased to prowl at night around the fold,
For sharper worries preyed upon their minds;
The timid roe and flying stag made friends
With hounds and wandered all around the farms.
The brood of the mighty sea was washed ashore
Like flotsam from a shipwreck, and the seals
Escaped to unfamiliar inland streams.
The viper died defenseless in her lair
And water snakes, their scales erect in fear.
Birds found the air too heavy for their wings
And, plunging earthward, left their lives aloft.
Change of pasture made no difference
And remedies effected only harm;
The masters of the healing arts gave up.
Pale Fury, flown from Hell's dark depths to the light,
Tisiphone, drove on Disease and Fear,
Her greedy head rose higher every day.
The bleating of the herds, their steady moans,
Filled all the river beds and thirsty banks,

Reverberating through the supine hills.
The Fury dealt out multitudinous deaths,
Heaping up cadavers in the stalls,
Rotting corpses stank and putrefied,
Until at last men buried them in pits.
The hides were useless, and the flesh so foul
That fire and water could not salvage it;
None could shear the fleece, nor touch the web.
If someone tried to wear the loathsome cloth,
He burned and blistered, rank repulsive sweat
Poured off his fetid limbs; and, soon enough,
His stricken body felt the sacred fire.

BOOK FOUR

Now I praise the honey heaven sends:
May this part too, Maecenas, please your eye.
I shall portray for you a marvelous scene;
A perfect, model state: its noble chiefs,
The nation's traits, pursuits, its wars and tribes.
The task is slight; its glory nothing small
If gods permit and Apollo hears my prayer.

First, find a settled dwelling for your bees
Away from wind (for breezes hinder them
In bringing home their food), where sheep and kids
Cannot abuse the flowers, nor straying calves
Brush off the dew and bruise the tender grass.
Keep spangled lizards far from your fertile hives,
The bee-devouring birds, like the swallow, Procne,
Whose bloodstained hands left marks upon her breast;
For all these birds play havoc with the bees
And pick them off in flight, to carry home
A tempting morsel for their clamoring young.
Find a spot where running springs abound
And moss-green pools, and where a slender brook

Slips through the grass, where palm trees or wild olives
Cast shade across the entrance, that in Spring
When new king bees lead out the earliest swarms
To frolic in their freedom from the combs,
A nearby bank may lure them from the heat,
A tree give leafy shelter in their path.
Halfway across the pond or running stream,
Place heavy rocks and willow boughs, for piers
Where the bees may stop to dry their moistened wings
In the Summer sun, if by chance a Southeast squall
Has drenched some stragglers or plunged them in the
    drink.
Plant laurels all around, and fragrant thyme;
Set out a crop of pungent savory,
And violet beds to drink the trickling spring.
    The hives you stitch from hollow bark, or weave
From pliant osier, need a narrow door:
For winter thickens honey with its cold
While summer liquefies and makes it run—
The bees dread both extremes, and sensibly
They smear the chinks with wax, fill crevices
With juice of flowers, and keep in store a glue
That binds more fast than Eastern pitch or bird-lime.
And often, if we may believe the tale,
They burrow underground to make their homes,

And will be found deep inside porous stones
Or in the hollow shell of rotten trees.
Smooth off the creviced chambers well with clay,
Arrange thin rows of leaves across the top.
Do not allow the yew to grow nearby,
Do not roast crimson crabs on your hearth; distrust
A deep marsh, any place where mud smells rank,
Or where the hollow rocks send bouncing back
The image of a voice that clangs against them.

When the golden sun drives Winter underground,
And Summer's light unlocks the sky, at once
The bees swarm out across the woods and groves
To harvest bright-hued flowers and drink from streams.
With some strange joy they form their children's nests,
Fashion new wax cleverly, and shape
The clinging honey. Glancing up, you see
Their column float through the crystal Summer air,
And marvel at their dense-dark windborne cloud:
Behold their tireless quest for pure fresh water,
Sheltering leaves. I urge you, sprinkle round
Scents of crushed balm leaf and honeywort;
Then make a din, and clink the Mother's cymbals:
The bees will settle down on the scented seats,
And hide in the cradling cells, as their custom is.

But if they go to fight—between two kings

Discord often stalks with heavy stride—
You can tell in advance, the mob has been aroused
And their hearts are pounding fearfully for war;
A brassy martial blare speeds stragglers on
As a sound is heard like fractured trumpet tones;
Excitedly they mass, with flashing wings,
Whet their stings on beaks, and flex their limbs,
Close in around the kings' tents, form their ranks,
And challenge the foe with mighty battle cries.
So on a dry Spring day in an open field
They burst the gates; they meet; the noise grows loud;
They mesh in a mighty sphere, then plunge straight
      down
Thicker than driven hail or a pelting shower
Of acorns rattled loose from the scarlet-oak.

   In the battle's midst, the chiefs with splendid wings
Display great courage in their tiny hearts.
Each one refusing stubbornly to yield
Before the other turns his back in flight.
This tide of animosity and strife
The keepers still with one handful of dust.

   Now when you've called both leaders from the front,
Dispatch the worst, to save yourself the burden,
And let the better rule the vacant court.
His golden-clustered coat of mail flares out;

Two kinds there are: the one of noble mien
Shines bright with flashing scales, the grisly one
Reveals ignoble sloth in his dragging paunch.
    As the kings have two aspects, so have the plebs:
The worse are as unsightly as a man
Who looms up in a swirling cloud of dust,
Parched and hot from walking, spitting dirt.
The others gleam and flash most splendidly,
Their bodies blaze, flecked evenly with gold.
From this more fecund breed, in heaven's sure time,
You draw off honey sweet, yet not so sweet
As crystal clear, that mellows hard-edged wine.
    But when the swarm flits aimlessly abroad,
Shuns the hive and lets the home grow cold,
Constrain their minds to cease the silly game.
The task's not hard: you pluck the king bee's wings;
With him at home, no other ventures out
Or dares to flaunt the guidons forth from camp.
Let gardens sweet with saffron lure them on,
And let Priapus's well-known guardianship
Keep thieves and birds at bay with his willow hook.
Let the keeper bring wild thyme and mountain laurel,
To plant in generous rows about their homes;
Let hard work leave its mark upon his hands
Who plants the slips and pours the welcome rains.

Indeed, if I were not now near the end
Of work, in haste to furl the sails and turn
The prow toward land, I'd sing of all the care
We spend on dressing fertile garden-plots,
Of Paestum's roses blooming twice a year,
Of riversides where endive loves to drink,
Of green-banked celery, how the curling gourd
Swells out its paunch and winds off into grass;
Nor would I fail to mention the narcissus
Flowering late, the curved acanthus' stem,
Pale ivy, and the myrtles' love of shores.
For I recall the towers of Tarentum,
Where black Galaesus waters yellow fields:
There once I saw an old man from Corycia,
With a patch of unclaimed land allotted him,
Not suitable for pasture, crops or wine.
This farmer, spacing herbs among his thickets,
And setting out white lilies, slender poppies,
And vervain, felt sure that his riches matched
The wealth of kings, when he came home at night
And heaped his table high with unbought foods.
He plucked the first Spring rose, the first Fall fruits;
And when the sullen Winter still hung on,
Bursting rocks with cold, and reining in
With ice the running streams, he went to clip

Soft strands of hyacinth and railed aloud
At Summer's tardy pace and the laggard winds.
His bees increased, his swarms were the most prolific,
He first drew honey foam from his close-packed hives.
His lime trees were luxuriant, like his pines:
For every orchard blossom in the Spring
The ripe trees bore a fruit at harvest time.
He set in rows his elms when well along,
Pear trees already hard, and blackthorn sloes,
Planes large enough to offer drinkers shade.
But I pass on, confined to narrow bounds,
And leave the rest for others after me.

   Now come, while I describe the character
Jove himself gave bees as recompense
For feeding heaven's king in his Cretan cave,
Where they followed the priests' loud chants and tin-
   kling brass.
Their children are common property; they share,
As partners, the city's dwelling, and live their lives
Under majestic laws. This species, solely,
Has a homeland, is sure of its household gods.
They work in summer, planning for the cold,
And store their gatherings in a common place.
Some organize for food and by consent
Are put to work in fields; inside the fort,

Still others lay foundations for the combs,
Formed of narcissus-tear and resin glue,
And hang on these the walls of clinging wax;
Others rear the young, their nation's hope;
And others press the pure transparent honey,
Filling cells to the brim with crystal nectar.
Some by lot are posted at the gates,
Where, taking turns, they watch for rain and clouds,
Or shoulder loads brought in, or close their ranks
Against the drones, to keep those idlers off.
The whole work hums along, the fragrant scent
Of honey tinged with thyme spreads through the air.
Like Cyclopean blacksmiths casting bolts
Of thunder, when they run in molten ore
And some with leather bellows ply the air
While others dip the hissing brass in troughs
And Etna groans beneath the anvil blows
As rhythmically their great arms rise and fall
Or turn the iron with tongs that grip it fast;
Like this, if small things may compare with great,
The spirit of possession drives the bees
To their respective tasks. The care of towns
Is given to the old, who wall the combs
And shape the chambers cunningly. The young
Return home late at night, their thighs hard-packed

With thyme—at random all day long they browse
Arbutus, laurel, willow, crimson crocus,
The rich lime blossom, russet hyacinth.
One time for all to rest from their achievements,
One time for all to labor, is the rule.
They rush out in the morning: no delay;
When evening warns them in from plain and pasture,
They make for home, restore their bodies' needs;
With murmuring sounds they buzz about the door-
        ways,
And settle in the cells as night draws on,
And silence reigns; sleep holds their weary limbs.
When rain impends, they stay close by their homes,
Refuse to trust the sky when East winds rise,
But, safely circling round the city walls,
They bring in water, making short sorties
And pick up pebbles, like unsteady skiffs
That take on ballast in a tossing sea,
And with these balance in the vaporous clouds.

   This custom of the bees may cause surprise:
They take no pleasure in the body's joys,
Nor melt away in love, nor bring to birth
Their young in labor; females pick their children
Straight from leaves, or gather them by mouth
From fragrant grass, maintaining by themselves

The royal line and tiny citizens,
Themselves rebuild the royal waxen realms.
They sometimes crush their wings on flinty rocks
In flight, and freely, while still burdened down,
Give up their lives: so strong in them is love
For flowers, so keen their pride in making honey.
And though their narrow life is quickly spanned
(They never last beyond the seventh year),
The race lives on, the household's fortune stands
Through many years and many generations.

   They serve their king more slavishly than Persians,
Than Parthia's people, Lydia's or Egypt's;
While he is safe, they all are of one mind;
If he is lost, they break their social bonds,
Steal the honey, raze the honeycombs.
He guides their progress, they look out for him,
All clamoring round, attending him in throngs.
They lift him to their shoulders and protect
Him with their bodies in the fray, and seek
Through fatal wounds the sacrifice of death.

   Some draw the implication from these facts
That bees possess divine intelligence
And drink of heaven's aether; they say that God
Extends throughout the whole expanse of sea,
Throughout the earth, throughout the depths of heaven;

That from him flocks and herds and men and beasts
Receive at birth the slender thread of life;
That thence all things return, to be dissolved,
And death is nowhere, since immortal souls
Soar aloft to join the starry throng.

   Now, if you will unseal their royal house,
Withdraw the honey from their treasuries:
Dash water on your body, rinse your mouth,
And take in hand a torch of piercing smoke.
Twice yearly men may reap the heavy harvest:
In May when the Pleiad lifts her noble face
Above the earth and spurns the Ocean's streams
Beneath her feet, and later in November
When she flees the rainy Fish in leaden sky
And drops, declining into Winter's waves.
Their wrath is overpowering, when attacked
The bees breathe poison in their bites, and leave
Their stingers fixed within the veins, and lay
Their lives beside them in the fatal wound.

   But if you pity them their ruined state
And humbled hearts, and want to spare the honey
For future use, in fear of cruel Winter—
Surely, you will fumigate the hives
With thyme, and cut away the empty cells?
For often, unobserved, the spotted newt

Gnaws at the combs, and swarms of skulking beetles
Crowd the house, and the empty-handed drone
Settles down to dine on others' food.
Fierce hornets bring superior armaments
Against the bees, or nasty moths get in,
Or spiders, those insects Minerva hates,
Suspend their sagging nets across the door.
But, all the lower down their fortunes sink
More eagerly they press to reconstruct
The ruins of their fallen race, and fill
The storied honeycombs, and weave again
The granaries they build from flower blossoms.
But if, since bees sustain vicissitudes
Like ours, their bodies languish in disease—
Infallibly you'll recognize the signs:
Straightway, their color alters, thin and drawn,
The haggard face contracts; they carry out
The dead remains of those whose light has failed,
In solemn funerals—and hanging, cling
About the door, or shut themselves inside,
Inert with hunger, idling, stupefied
By gripping chills. An ominous tone resounds,
Protracted buzzing, like the cold South Wind
Sighing through the forest, like the sea
When restlessly she ebbs with hissing waves,

Like roaring fire that licks at furnace doors.
My counsel is: to burn some scented gum,
And drip in honey down through pipes of reed,
And straightway urge the weary creatures on
To taste familiar food. A draft of juice
Distilled from apple gall and dried rose leaves
May be of help, or thick wine must, fermented
Over slow flame, or Psithian raisin wine,
Or Attic thyme and odored centaury.
A meadow flower farmers call "amellus"
Is found quite easily; from single stalks
A mass of shoots come up; the flower is golden,
Petals clustering thick around the bud
Are violet-dark and streaked with crimson light;
In woven wreaths it often decorates
Our sacred shrines; it leaves a bitter taste;
Among the well-cropped grasslands in our valleys
Shepherds pick this plant, beside the streams
Of Mella curving round through northern Brescia:
Boil amellus roots in scented wine,
And place the food in baskets by their doors.

 For the man whose swarm fails all at once, where none
Is left him to renew the stock, it is time
To tell the Arcadian master's famed resource,
The method long since used of breeding bees

From slaughtered bullocks' putrid blood. I'll tell
The story whole and trace the legend's source.
Where Macedonians colonized Canopus,
The favored race beside the Nile's slow flood
Who drive around their farms in painted boats—
The land the Persian archers press hard on,
Where the stream rolls down from India's swarthy
    tribes
Toward its separate mouths, to fertilize
Green Egypt with a rich black sandy loam—
The whole place finds success in this technique.

  A narrow site, restricted for this use,
Is chosen first; they wall it in, impose
A narrow arching roof, insert four windows
Sloping toward the winds for feeble light.
They find a two-year calf with sprouting horns
Whose nostrils and whose breathing mouth they stop,
Despite his struggles; beat and pulverize
The carcass, while they keep the skin intact.
Here enclosed they leave him, laying sticks
And sprays of thyme and new-cut cinnamon
Beneath his flanks. All this is done
When West winds ruffle Ocean's waves in Spring,
Before the meadows bloom in bright new colors,
Before the chattering swallow hangs her nest

In raftered barns. Meanwhile, within the corpse
The fluids heat, the soft bones tepefy,
And creatures fashioned wonderfully appear;
First void of limbs, but soon awhir with wings
They swarm; then more and more they try the thin air,
Until they at last break through, like rain poured down
From summer clouds, or like shafts from the quivering
    bow
When Parthian light-armed ranks make their first
    attack.
What god, O Muses, forged this art for us?
Who placed this new experience in our path?
The shepherd Aristaeus lost his swarm,
Our story goes, through hunger and disease,
And fled from Tempe toward the stream Peneus.
Beside the sacred head of the river's source
He stood disconsolate and told his tale
Of woes, addressed his mother in these words:
    "Mother, Cyrene mother, dwelling here
Within these swirling depths, why was I born
To suffer from the fates, if, as you say,
Apollo is my father, and I am
A member of the famous race of gods?
The love you had for me is banished—where?
Why did you once extend my hopes to heaven?

See, mother though you are, how I have lost
This crown of mortal life, experience
With bees that practice taught me, barely gained
Along with skill in tending herds and crops.
Uproot then with your hands my fruitful trees,
Bring on your hostile fire against my barns,
Lay my harvest low, consume my crops,
And wield a ruthless axe against my vines,
Since all my praise has bred disgust in you."
  His mother in her river room below
Heard the sound. Around her sat the nymphs
All spinning Milesian wool dyed glossy-green;
Drymo, Xantho, Phyllodoce, Ligea,
Whose dazzling hair flows round their snow-white
    necks;
Cydippe, golden-haired Lycorias,
The first a maiden still, the other then
Acquainted with the labors of first birth;
Beroe, Clio, Ocean's daughters both,
Both clad in gold and varicolored skins;
Ephyre, Opis, Asian Deiopea;
Swift Arethusa, now returned from the chase.
Among them, Clymene was holding forth
On Vulcan's baffled love, the stolen sweets
And tricks of Mars, relating the countless loves

Of all the gods from Chaos to the present.
Entranced by her account, they spin the wool,
When Aristaeus' grief a second time
Strikes on his mother's ear, transfixing all
Upon their glossy chairs. Before the rest,
Arethusa raised her golden head
To look above the water's crest, and called:
"Cyrene, sister, such profound lament
Might well alarm you, for your protégé
Himself, your Aristaeus, stands beside
Father Peneus' wave, disconsolate
And tearful, citing you for cruelty."
    The mother, filled with unnamed dread, replied:
"Lead him down to us; he has the right
To touch the gods' threshold"; she then commands
The river's depths to yield the boy a path.
The curling wave arched round him like a mountain,
Enfolded him, and set him down below.
And now he viewed with awe his mother's home,
And paced the watery empire, walking round
The lakes locked inside caves, the resonant groves;
The powerful rush of water made him reel
To see the mighty rivers underground
All gliding in their separate directions:
The Phasis and the Lycus of Caucasia,

The Enipeus River's source in northern Greece,
And father Tiber's head, swift Anio's,
The Mandragora watering the Levant,
The Slavic Boug that roars across its rocks,
The bull-faced River Po with gilded horns,
Whose flow is most impetuous of all
That wind through fertile lands to the dark blue sea.
When Aristaeus reached his mother's room,
Its ceilings arched with vaults of porous stone,
Cyrene heard out his tale of idle tears;
The sisters poured fresh water on his hands,
And offered smooth wool towels, as is meet.
They spread a feast, replenished all the cups.
The mother spoke: "Now, take the goblets full
Of Lydian wine; we'll pour a drop to Ocean!"
Cyrene made her vows at once to Ocean,
Father of all, and to the sister nymphs
Who guard a hundred woods, a hundred streams.
Three times she spilled out on the blazing hearth
A draft of purest nectar, three times back
The flame shot glancing upward off the ceiling:
Encouraged by the omen, she began:

   "A sea-blue prophet dwells in the Aegean,
Proteus, who rides the mighty deep behind
A string of fish and brace of water-horses.

At present, he is looking in on ports
In Thessaly and his native land, Pallene.
We nymphs and ancient Nereus praise this seer
For, as a prophet, he knows everything,
What is, what has been, what is soon to come.
It pleased Neptune to grant the gift to him,
For Proteus tends the monsters of the deep
And feeds the ugly seals beneath the waves.
Now, son, first capture Proteus and chain him,
That he divulge the reason for your plague
And show its cure. But he will not give counsel
Until forced: for words he'll not relent.
So bind him fast with force and chains, and then
His tricks will clash against their bonds in vain.
I'll lead you to the place the old man hides
When the sun enkindles flaming heat at noon,
When grass is parched and cattle seek the shade.
You'll steal upon him as he lies asleep,
Tired from his morning's journey with the waves.
But when you have him anchored down with chains,
He'll alter into various forms of beast:
First to savage boar, then to jet-black tiger,
To scaly dragon, tawny lioness;
Or, hissing like greedy flame, he slips the bounds
Or dissolves into vaporous flood and so makes off.

But all the more the shapes that he assumes
Hold on, my son, and draw the chains more tight,
Until once more he turns back to the form
He had at first when sleep obscured his sight."
   She poured ambrosial fragrance on her son
That seeped through every corner of his frame;
His shapely locks exhaled the gentle savor
And supple strength found ways to seize his limbs.
There lies a deep cave, hollowed in a mountain
Where wind-driven waves break into harmless parts,
In former times a safe and sure retreat
For storm-tossed mariners: inside this cave
Proteus hid behind a jutting rock.
Cyrene brought the shepherd to the spot,
Concealed him in the shadows out of view
And drew off at a distance, wrapped in cloud.
   The pitiless Dog Star blazed away in heaven
Roasting India's parched inhabitants,
The fiery sun had used up half his course,
The grass lay scorched, the heat rays baked and cooked
On the hollow streams' dried channels and mud-bed.
And now old Proteus coming in from sea
Made for his usual haunt within the cave.
Round him frisked the damp tribes of the deep,
Sprinkling far and wide the bitter brine.

Sleepy seals stretched out along the shore,
While he, like some old shepherd of the hills
Who leads his flock at evening to the barns
(Wolves lick their chops at the sound of the bleating
    lambs),
Sits on a rock in their midst and counts them over.
Now that occasion favored Aristaeus
He barely let the old man fall asleep
And rest his weary limbs, before he swooped
On the lying hulk with a shout, and chained it fast.
Proteus now, remembering all his tricks,
Transformed himself into most miraculous shapes
To fire, to fearful beast, to liquid flood.
But since no trick could save him, Proteus
Resumed his form and spoke with human voice:
"Oh rash young man, who sent you to our home?
What are you after here?" The boy replied:
"You know well, Proteus; don't pretend you don't.
Cease trying, then, to fool me. We have come,
Instructed by the gods, to seek from you
An oracle to restore our flagging fortunes."
He said this much. Then the prophet, bowing to force
Rolled his eyes ablaze with grey-green light
And gnashed his teeth as he released the fates:
"A god's wrath makes you pay this heavy price

(Though even this is less than you deserve)
And would make you still, did Fate not intervene:
Unhappy Orpheus roused this punishment,
Who rages still with grief for his stolen bride.
Headlong past a stream, the fated girl
In fleeing your advances, failed to see
The monstrous serpent lurking on the shore.
Her Dryads filled the mountain heights with moans;
Summits wept in Thrace and Macedon,
And in Rhesus' martial land; the Hebrus wept,
The Danube, and the fair princess of Athens.
Orpheus soothed his love with the hollow lyre,
Singing to thee, sweet bride, along the strand
Alone, with rising day and falling night.
He breached the jaws of Hell, the home of Dis,
The pitch-black groves of fear; approached the dead,
To win the frightful king, and all the hearts
That know not how to answer human prayer.
At his song, from Hell's deep places rustled forth
The slender shades of those whose light has failed,
Like birds that flock by thousands to the leaves
When Winter rain or nightfall sends them down
From mountainsides: the mothers and their husbands,
Noble heroes' bodies void of life,
Boys, unwedded girls, and youthful sons

Consigned to fire before their parents' eyes.
Around them wind Cocytus' twisted reeds
And grisly mud; the sluggish, hateful swamp
Confines them, as the ninefold swirling Styx
Encompasses them about. The very halls
Of Hell and inmost Tartarus stand open
In surprise; the Furies are astounded,
Their bluish tresses intertwined with snakes.
Cerberus, in amazement, holds his three
Mouths open, and even the wind subsides;
Ixion's wheel stands still. Now Orpheus had
Retraced his steps, avoiding all mischance,
Eurydice approached the upper air
Behind him (as Proserpina had ruled),
When all at once a mad desire possessed
The unwise lover—pardonable, indeed,
If Hell knew how to pardon. Overcome
By love, he stopped and—oh, forgetful man!—
Looked back at his, his own, Eurydice,
As they were drawing near the upper light.
That instant, all his labor went to waste,
His pact with the cruel tyrant fell apart,
And three times thunder rocked Avernus' swamps.
She cried out, 'What wild fury ruins us,
My pitiable self, and you, my Orpheus?

See, once again the cruel fates call me back
And once more sleep seals closed my swimming eyes.
Farewell: prodigious darkness bears me off,
Still reaching out to you these helpless hands
That you may never claim.' And with her words
She vanished from his sight like smoke in air,
Not seeing him clutch wildly after shadows
And yearning still to speak. Hell's ferryman
Refused him further passage through the swamp
That intervened. What could he do? Where turn,
A second time bereft of her? What tears
Might sway the dead, what human voice might alter
Heaven's will? Her body, stiff and cold,
Reposed long since adrift in the Stygian bark.
Seven continuous months, they say, he wept
By Strymon's lonely wave under soaring cliffs,
Unfolding his tragic song to the frozen stars,
Enchanting tigers, moving oaks with his theme:
Like a nightingale concealed in the poplar's shade,
Who sings a sad lament for her stolen brood
Some stony-hearted ploughman saw and dragged
Still naked from the nest: she weeps all night
And, perching on the bough, renews her song
Of elegiac woe; her grave complaint
Fills places far and wide. No thought of love

Or wedding rites could bend his inflexible will.
He wandered lonely through the icy North,
Past the snow-encrusted Don, through mountain fields
Of unadulterated frost, conveyed the grief
At Hell's ironic offerings, and rapt
Eurydice. By such unwavering faith
The Thracian women felt themselves outraged,
And at their sacred exercise, nocturnal
Bacchanals, they tore the youth apart,
And scattered his limbs around the spacious fields.
But even then his voice, within the head
Torn from its marble neck, and spinning down
The tide of his paternal River Hebrus,
The cold-tongued voice itself, as life fled away,
Called out 'Oh, my forlorn Eurydice!
Eurydice!' and the shoreline answered back
Along the river's breadth, 'Eurydice!' "

    With these words, Proteus plunged back in the deep
And where he dove, the water swirled with foam.
Cyrene stayed, and addressed her startled son:
"My son, dismiss your worries from your mind.
This was the plague's whole cause, for this the Nymphs
With whom she danced far into woodland groves
Devised your bees' bleak end. Entreat their peace
By humbly offering gifts, and venerate

The gracious Dryads; they will pardon you,
Repress their wrath in favor of your vows.
I'll tell you first precisely how to pray:
Select the four best bullocks from the herd
Now grazing on Arcadia's verdant crest.
And choose four matching heifers, still unbroken.
By the goddesses' lofty shrines erect four altars,
Where the sacred blood may trickle from their throats,
And leave the creatures' hulks in a shady grove.
When the ninth succeeding Dawn displays her course
You'll send to Orpheus, as his funeral dues,
Oblivion's poppies: slay a jet-black ewe,
And find the grove again; and sacrifice
A calf to reconcile Eurydice."

   Without delay he does his mother's bidding,
Comes to the shrine, creates the altars there
That she prescribed; selects his four best steers,
Leads in four matching heifers, still unbroken.
When the ninth succeeding Dawn led on her course,
He sent off Orpheus' due and found the grove.
Here a wonder strange to tell appears,
When from the bellies, over the rotten flesh
Of the corpses, bees buzz out from caved-in flanks,
Swarm in heavy clouds to treetops, group,
And hang in clusters down from the pliant boughs.

* * * *

All this I've sung of cultivating fields,
Of tending flocks and caring for the trees,
While by the deep Euphrates noble Caesar
Thunders triumph, grants the reign of law
To grateful subjects, clears his path to heaven.
All this time sweet Naples nourished me,
Her Virgil, in the flower of humble peace,
In study: I who played at shepherds' songs
In callow youth, and sang, O Tityrus,
Of you at ease beneath your spreading beech.